Ōlim nce upon a time...IN LATIN

DERIVATIVES
BOOK I

CONCEIVED & WRITTEN
BY MARY ELLEN TEDROW-WYNN

EDITED BY SUSAN SCHEARER

ILLUSTRATIONS BY RACHEL SCHANZENBACH

COVER, LAYOUT DESIGN, & TYPESETTING BY ALLISON ARMERDING

We have checked for errors in this text.

However, should you notice any mistakes, we would love to hear from you.

Please contact us at *laurelwoodbooks@earthlink.net*.

Ōlim Derivatives Book I

Laurelwood Books © 2015

ISBN: 978-1-941383-21-6

Find this and other great books on our website:

www.laurelwoodbooks.com

You may also reach us at:

Laurelwood Books

1639 Ebenezer Road

Bluemont, VA 20135

Notes for the Teacher

Welcome to Derivatives I! This series can stand alone or be used alongside any Latin program. Vocabulary has been taken from the *Ōlim, Once Upon a Time in Latin* series. Using it in conjunction with the *Ōlim* series will help with vocabulary retention. Although this book is written for fifth or sixth graders, it can be used by younger and older students.

Don't rush through Derivatives. We recommend that you and your students take two weeks to complete the exercises in each Lesson. For example:

Week I

    Day 1: Trace Latin and English words, note Derivatives*

    Day 2: Exercise I: Fill in the Blank

    Day 3: Exercise II: Matching

    Day 4: Exercise III: Story with Blanks

Week 2

    Day 5: Exercise IV: Multiple Choice

    Day 6: Exercise V: Write Your Own Story

    Day 7: Crossword or Word Search Puzzle

    Extras: Write Derivatives (every five lessons)

*When copying Latin words, be sure to add <u>macrons</u>. Macrons are the diacritical mark indicating a long vowel in Latin. Example: duōs.

Each lesson introduces 10 Latin vocabulary words.

- <u>Verbs</u>, marked by (v), appear in the infinitive, usually followed by other forms (third person present, third person past, etc.)
- <u>Nouns</u>, marked by (n), generally appear with the singular (s) and plural (pl) forms.
- <u>Adjectives</u>, marked (adj), appear with three endings. Why? Because in Latin, adjective endings must match the nouns they modify in gender (masculine, feminine, neuter), in number (singular, plural) and in case (nominative, accusative, dative, genitive, ablative).

How to Pronounce Latin

a	ah	the first syllable of "aha"	
		with a macron, twice as long, as in 2nd syllable of "aha"	portābat
ae	eye	as in "line"	Graeciae
au	ow	as in "how"	causa
b	b	normal English	
c	k	as in "kick"	Cicero
d	d	normal English	
e	eh	as in "met"	
		with a macron: AY as in "make" or "day"	petēbat
ei	AY	as in "make" or "day"	deinde
			(NOT de-inde)
eu	eoo	as in "you" (but without the strong "y"); "ew, that stinks!"	Eurōpa
f	f	normal English	
g		hard g as in "game" (NOT as in "germ")	gerere
h		breathe out (Latin considers this neither a vowel nor a consonant)	
i + consonant OR inside a word: ih, as in "hit"			
		with a macron: EE as in "feet"	dīcit
i followed by a vowel at the beginning of a word "y" as in "yard"			iam
j		sometimes used for "i followed by a vowel at the beginning of a word"	
			Jūlius = Iūlius
k		used only in Latin words borrowed from Greek; pronounced as English "k"	
l, m, n	normal English		
o		as in "port"	
		with macron "oh" as in "hello"	optō
oe	oy	as in "toy"	foedus
p	p	normal English	
qu	kw	as in "quick"	quisque
r	r	normal English	
s	s	as in "see" (NO "z" sound)	Āsia
t	t	normal English	
u	uh	as in "us"	
		with macron "oo" as in "shoe"	Iūlius
ui	wi	as in "queen"	cui
			(yes, this sounds just like quī)
v	w	as in "with"	Salvē
w		did not exist in Latin	
x	ks	normal English	
y	euh	somewhere between a short "i" and a short "u"	Syra
z		did not exist in Latin; borrowed from Greek's zeta, as in zephyrus.	

How to Pronounce Latin

Pronounce double letters TWICE:

"cc" as in "kicK Kings"   "nn" as in "oN Nothing"

"ff" as in "ofF First"   "pp" as in "uP Periscope"

"gg" as in "doG Game"   "ss" as in "aS Seems"

"ll" as in "alL Lost"   "tt" as in "ducT Tape"

"mm" as in "I'M Messy"

SYLLABLES AND ACCENTS:

1) A syllable is determined by having a vowel or diphthong (two vowels pronounced as one, as in ae, au, ei, eu, oe, ui: see the list above)

The third-to-last syllable is the *antepenult*.

The next-to-last syllable is the *penult*.

The last syllable is the *ultima*.

2) Accent the penult in a two-syllable word: *Amat*

3) Accent the penult in a 3-or-more-syllable word IF the penult

-- has a macron: *puelLĀrum*

-- OR ends in two consonants: *puELla*

4) Otherwise accent antepenult: *AMbulat*

Roman Numerals

I = 1	XVI = 16	XXXI = 31	XLVI = 46
II = 2	XVII = 17	XXXII = 32	XLVII = 47
III = 3	XVIII = 18	XXXIII = 33	XLVIII = 48
IV = 4	XIX = 19	XXXIV = 34	XLIX = 49
V = 5	XX = 20	XXXV = 35	L = 50
VI = 6	XXI = 21	XXXVI = 36	LI = 51
VII = 7	XXII = 22	XXXVII = 37	LII = 52
VIII = 8	XXIII = 23	XXXVIII = 38	LIII = 53
IX = 9	XXIV = 24	XXXIX = 39	LIV = 54
X = 10	XXV = 25	XL = 40	LV = 55
XI = 11	XXVI = 26	XLI = 41	LVI = 56
XII = 12	XXVII = 27	XLII = 42	LVII = 57
XIII = 13	XXVIII = 28	XLIII = 43	LVIII = 58
XIV = 14	XXIX = 29	XLIV = 44	LIX = 59
XV = 15	XXX = 30	XLV = 45	LX = 60

LESSON I: Vocabulary

Study these Latin words, their meanings, and their English derivatives.

LATIN WORD	MEANING	DERIVATIVES
1. dicere, dīcit, dīxit (v)	to say, (he) says, (he) said	diction dictionary
2. prīmus, prīma, prīmum (adj)	first	primary premier
3. exīre (v)	to go out, exit	exit
4. magnus, magna, magnum (adj)	large	magnify magnificent magnavox
5. portāre, portō, portat (v)	to carry, I carry, (he) carries	porter transport portable
6. malus, mala, malum (adj)	bad	malicious maleficent malice malaria malodorous
7. velle, volō, volunt (v)	to want, I want, they want	voluntary volunteer
8. videre, videt, vidit (v)	to see, (he) sees, (he) saw	video vision supervise provide evident visible revise provision providence
9. trēs, trēs, tria (adj)	three	triangle triple trilogy tripod triplet trio
10. māter (n)	mother	maternity maternal

	Trace the Latin vocabulary words, meanings, and English derivatives below. Then add macrons!		
1	Word & Meaning:	dicere, dicit, dixit	to say, (he) says, (he) said
	Derivatives:	diction, dictionary	
2	Word & Meaning:	primus, prima, primum	first
	Derivatives:	primary, premier	
3	Word & Meaning:	exire	to go out, exit
	Derivatives:	exit	
4	Word & Meaning:	magnus, magna, magnum	large
	Derivatives:	magnify, magnificent, magnavox	
5	Word & Meaning:	portare, portat	to carry, (he) carries
	Derivatives:	porter, transport, portable	
6	Word & Meaning:	malus, mala, malum	bad
	Derivatives:	malicious, maleficent, malice	
		malaria, malodorous	
7	Word & Meaning:	velle, volo, volunt	to want, I want, they want
	Derivatives:	voluntary, volunteer	
8	Word & Meaning:	videre, videt, vidit	to see, (he) sees, (he) saw
	Derivatives:	video, vision, supervise, provide, evident	
		visible, revise, provision, providence	
9	Word & Meaning:	tres, tres, tria	three
	Derivatives:	triangle, triple, trilogy	
		triplet, trio	
10	Word & Meaning:	mater	mother
	Derivatives:	maternity, maternal	

LESSON I: Exercise I

Complete the sentences using English Derivatives.

FILL IN THE BLANK

1. To find out the meaning of a word, we look in a
____dictionary____.

2. Someone who carries luggage is a____porter____.

3. To make something look larger, we
____Magnify____it.

4. When speaking, I should use good____diction____.

5. He was such a____Malicious____person,
he went to jail.

6. He went through the door to____exit____
the building.

7. English is his____primary____language.

8. He plans to____Volunteer____at the homeless
shelter.

9. She wants to take a____Video____
of the birthday party.

10. In geometry, we study the sides and angles of a
____triangle____.

CHOICES

exit

primary

diction

magnify

porter

malicious

volunteer

video

dictionary

triangle

LESSON I: Exercise II

Use a ruler. Draw a line to match the English derivative to its Latin word.

DERIVATIVE

LATIN WORD

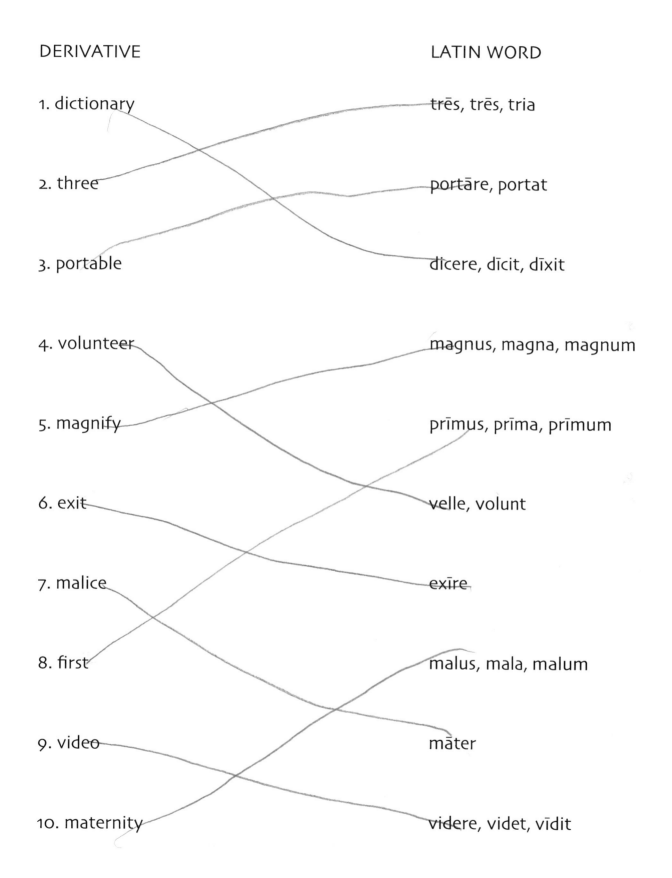

1. dictionary

2. three

3. portable

trēs, trēs, tria

portāre, portat

dīcere, dīcit, dīxit

4. volunteer

5. magnify

6. exit

7. malice

8. first

9. video

10. maternity

magnus, magna, magnum

prīmus, prīma, prīmum

velle, volunt

exīre

malus, mala, malum

māter

vidēre, videt, vīdit

LESSON I: Exercise III

Fill in the blanks using English derivatives. Your choices are listed at the bottom of the page.

STORY

Our family went on a trip. The 1)_____

carried our bags. He was from another country, but spoke with good

2)_____.

One bag was very 3)_____. He dropped it

by accident. We knew it wasn't done with 4)_____.

Our mother said to give him a tip because this is his job. He is not a

5)_____.

CHOICES

large	volunteer	porter	malice	diction

LESSON I: Exercise IV

What does the underlined word mean? Circle your choice.

1. It is the <u>primary</u> reason for doing it.

    a) only   b) wrong   c) first

2. I want to <u>magnify</u> the picture.

    a) burn   b) change it   c) make it larger

3. The suitcase is <u>portable</u>.

    a) very heavy   b) able to be carried   c)wet

4. She had a <u>malicious</u> attitude.

    a) happy   b) bad   c) goofy

5. The teacher drew a <u>triangle</u> on the board.

    a) 30-sided shape   b) four-sided shape   c) three-sided shape

6. The man <u>volunteers</u> at the shop.

    a) offers to help   b) goes to   c) drives to

7. The <u>maternal</u> feelings came naturally to the girl.

    a) happy   b) motherly   c) mixed-up

LESSON I: Exercise V

Write a story using as many words from this lesson as you can. Underline the words you use.

_____

_____

_____

_____

_____

_____

_____

_____

_____

_____

_____

_____

_____

_____

_____

_____

LESSON I: Exercise VI

Circle the English derivatives in the puzzle below.

```
M X R Y R U S R R O X X Q S X Y H S J S
A B V D I X G U D Y I O A Y R J T A O P
T N N A B W M B P H W M G U F V L H A R
E B W V U T A N E E W U L C J B V D T E
R V Q E C R T W U K R R V H Y B E I R M
N O P E P I E V P S U V M M M Y J C A I
A L H V K A R Z R M B V I X J V P T N E
L U S I V N N Y A C E T S O H R I S R
N N Q D V G I O J L A X R L E B I O P G
Z T Z E L L T K T O I S I M Q E M N O I
D E T N A L Y V Y D C S O Z K X A A R V
M E Z T I B Y G F O F F T S I U R R T M
A R K J W W V Y C R K W P L E A Y Y R Y
G Z Z C O P B P R O V I D E N C E X I Y
N P H N U K E P I U I D O P Z Q G F L H
I O M C U G S O C S E B V K Q L X N O W
F D U C W G S G E A X Q V G A V K J G P
Y T V I S I B L E Z I Y K J R Q E K Y E
P U M A L A R I A V T P O R T E R H V E
T E E X R G M A L I C I O U S J D D H L
```

MALODOROUS
TRANSPORT
PREMIER
MALICIOUS
EXIT
TRIO
MAGNIFY

EVIDENT
PROVIDENCE
SUPERVISE
TRILOGY
MATERNAL
DICTIONARY
PRIMARY

VOLUNTEER
PORTER
MALARIA
MATERNITY
VISIBLE
TRIANGLE

LESSON II: Vocabulary

Study these Latin words, their meanings, and their English derivatives.

Latin Word	Meaning	Derivatives	
1. intrāre, intrat (v)	to enter, (he) enters	introduce entrance	
2. necesse	necessary	necessary	
3. porcus (s), porcī (pl) (n)	pig, pigs	pork porcupine porpoise	
4. prūdēns, prūdentēs	wise (comes from *pro videntes*--"seeing ahead of time")	prudent	
5. respondere, respondet, respondit (v)	to respond/answer, (he) responds/answers, (he) responded/answered	respond correspond responsible response	
6. venīre, venit, vēnit (v)	to come, (he) comes, (he) came	Advent adventure venture intervene	prevent convention convent invent
7. vīlla (n)	house	villa village villain	
8. currere, currit (v)	to run, (he) runs	precursor current cursor occur	recur incur currency
9. rapidissimus, rapidissima, rapidissimum (adj)	very fast	rapid	
10. audīre, audit (v)	to hear, (he) hears	auditory audience auditorium audible audition	

		Trace the Latin vocabulary words, meanings, and English derivatives below. Then add macrons!
1	Word & Meaning:	intrare, intrat to enter, (he) enters
	Derivatives:	introduce, entrance
2	Word & Meaning:	necesse necessary
	Derivatives:	necessary
3	Word & Meaning:	porcus, porci pig, pigs
	Derivatives:	pork, porcupine, porpoise
4	Word & Meaning:	prudens, prudentes wise
	Derivatives:	prudent
5	Word & Meaning:	respondere, respondet, respondit
		to respond,/answer, (he) responds/answers,
		(he) responded/answered
	Derivatives:	respond, correspond, responsible, response
6	Word & Meaning:	venire, venit, venit
		to come, (he) comes, (he) came
	Derivatives:	Advent, adventure, venture, intervene, prevent
		convention, convent, invent
7	Word & Meaning:	villa house
	Derivatives:	villa, village, villain
8	Word & Meaning:	currere, currit to run, (he) runs
	Derivatives:	precursor, current, cursor, occur, recur, incur, currency
9	Word & Meaning:	rapidissimus, rapidissima, rapidissimum
		very fast
	Derivatives:	rapid
10	Word & Meaning:	audire, audit to hear, (he) hears
	Derivatives:	auditory, audience, auditorium, audible, audition

LESSON II: Exercise I

Complete the sentences using English Derivatives.

FILL IN THE BLANK   CHOICES

1. If you want to meet someone, you should   pork

_____yourself.
                                                                    respond

2. To learn, it is_____to study!
                                                                    necessary

3. Mom is cooking_____ BBQ
for dinner tonight.   auditorium

4. When someone asks you a question, you should   introduce

_____.

5. We heard the speaker in a huge   Advent

_____.
                                                                    prudent

6. Be _____when you must make   village
a decision.

                                                                    current

7. Sometimes the_____ in the
ocean is very strong.

8. They lived in a small _____.

9. The season before Christmas is called

_____.

LESSON II: Exercise II

Use a ruler. Draw a line to match the English derivative to its Latin word.

DERIVATIVE	LATIN WORD
1. necessary	respondere
2. pork, porcupine, porpoise	venīre
3. respond	currere
4. adventure	necesse
5. house	porcus, porcī
6. current	rapidissimus, -a, -um
7. rapid	vīlla
8. introduce	audīre
9. prudent	intrāre
10. auditorium	prūdēns

LESSON II: Exercise III

Fill in the blanks using English derivatives. Your choices are listed at the bottom of the page.

STORY

My friend is having a party. He sent out invitations and I sent a

1)_____. They live in a large

2)_____. I don't know some of the other people

so I will 3)_____ myself.

The mom said it was not 4)_____ to bring a gift. I am

bringing one anyway. They are serving 5)_____

BBQ and coleslaw. Mmm, I love those! It will be 6)_____

of me not to eat too much.

We went swimming in the river behind their house. Even though the

7)_____ was strong, everyone stayed safe and had a

good time.

_____

CHOICES

introduce   current   response   pork   prudent   necessary   villa

LESSON II: Exercise IV

What does the underlined word mean? Circle your choice.

1. We stayed at the <u>villa</u> overnight.

    a) barn   b) house   c) show

2. It was <u>necessary</u> to go.

    a) hard   b) easy   c) required, must do it

3. We lit candles during <u>Advent</u>, the season before...

    a) Easter   b) Thanksgiving   c) Christmas

4. You see an <u>audiologist</u> in order to be tested for your...

    a) hearing   b) surgeon   c) podiatrist

5. The _____ had prickly quills.

    a) beaver   b) porcupine   c) giraffe

6. When making a decision, one should be <u>prudent</u>.

    a) silly   b) wise   c) sad

LESSON II: Exercise V

Write a story using as many words from this lesson as you can. Underline the words you use.

_____

_____

_____

_____

_____

_____

_____

_____

_____

_____

_____

_____

_____

_____

_____

LESSON II: Exercise VI

Choose <u>English derivatives</u> to solve the puzzle below. (Latin words are in parentheses.)

DOWN

1) an evil character (vīlla)
2) able to be heard (audīre)
4) needed (necesse)
5) a whale with a round snout (porcus)
6) a country's system of money (currere)

ACROSS

3) to create or design (venīre)
7) fast (rapidissimus)
8) wise (prūdēns)
9) having an obligation to do something (respondere)
10) to make known (intrāre)

LESSON III: Vocabulary

Study these Latin words, their meanings, and their English derivatives.

LATIN WORD	MEANING	DERIVATIVES	
1. prōvocāre, prōvocat (v.)	to challenge, (he) challenges	provoke provocation provoked	
2. cursus (n.)	a race	course precursor cursive	excursion concourse
3. superāre, superat (v.)	to overcome, (he) overcomes	superior superman superlative supervise supersede (sit above)	
4. cēterī, cēterae, cētera (adj)	all the others	et cetera (and all the others)	
5. animāl, animālia (n)	animal, animals	animals animation	
6. silva (n)	forest	Pennsylvania (Penn's woods) sylvan	
7. excitāre, excitat (v)	to excite, (he) excites	excitement incite	
8. initium	beginning, start	initially initial initials	
9. alter, altera, alterum (adj)	another	alters alteration alter ego alternate alternative	
10. ūnus, ūna, ūnum (adj)	one	unity union united unison university unicycle	

		Trace the Latin vocabulary words, meanings, and English derivatives below. Then add macrons!	
1	Word & Meaning:	provocare, provocat	to challenge, (he) challenges
	Derivatives:	provoke, provocation, provoked	
2	Word & Meaning:	cursus	a race
	Derivatives:	course, precursor, cursive, excursion, concourse	
3	Word & Meaning:	superare, superat	to overcome, (he) overcomes
	Derivatives:	superior, superman, superlative, supervise, supersede	
4	Word & Meaning:	ceteri, ceterae, cetera	all the others
	Derivatives:	et cetera (etc.)	
5	Word & Meaning:	animal, animalia	animal, animals
	Derivatives:	animals, animation	
6	Word & Meaning:	silva	forest
	Derivatives:	Pennsylvania, sylvan	
7	Word & Meaning:	excitare, excitat	to excite, (he) excites
	Derivatives:	excitement, incite	
8	Word & Meaning:	initium	beginning, start
	Derivatives:	initially, initial, initials	
9	Word & Meaning:	alter, altera, alterum	another
	Derivatives:	alters, alteration, alter ego, alternate, alternative	
10	Word & Meaning:	unus, una, unum	one
	Derivatives:	unity, union, united, unison, university, unicycle	

LESSON III: Exercise I

Complete the sentences using English Derivatives.

FILL IN THE BLANK   CHOICES

1. Tom Daly's _____ are TD.   provoke

2. Johnny planned to take a _____   course
   in algebra.

3. We used that book before. We need an   Superman

   _____ .   et cetera

4. Dad said, "Don't_____
   your sister."   animals

5. We saw many_____   Pennsylvania
   in the zoo.

6._____ means "Penn's woods."   excited

7._____can leap over tall   initials
   buildings.

8. We live in the_____States .   alternative,
                                                             alternate

9. The children were so_____they screamed.   United

10. We ordered pansies, petunias, lilies, daisies,

_____.

LESSON III: Exercise II

Use a ruler. Draw a line to match the English derivative to its Latin word.

DERIVATIVE

LATIN WORD

1. animal

superāre

2. course

excitāre, excitat, excitābat

3. initials, initial

animāl

4. one

cēterī, cēterae, cētera

5. superman

cursus

6. excite

silva

7. et cetera

alter, altera, alterum

8. to provoke, he provokes, provoked

initium

9. alternative, alternate

ūnus, ūna, ūnum

10. Pennsylvania

prōvocare, prōvocat, prōvocāvit

LESSON III: Exercise III

Fill in the blanks using English derivatives. Your choices are listed at the bottom of the page.

STORY

Susan decided to take part in the race. The 1)_____

was set. 2)_____ (at the beginning), she was

cold. She was 3)_____ to wear a sweatshirt

with her brother's number on it.

There were two different routes to take. At first all runners were

4)_____. Then some took the 5)_____

route. When Susan won, even the 6)_____

in the 7)_____ were happy.

CHOICES

forest   initially   course   alternate   excited   animals   united

LESSON III: Exercise IV

What does the underlined word mean? Circle your choice.

1. We knew there was more to the sentence because it ended "et cetera."

    a) and the others   b) be happy   c) do more

2. Her initial response was sadness.

    a) later   b) first   c) last

3. He was provoked to do the right thing.

    a) told   b) warned   c) challenged

4. The manager chose an alternative plan.

    a) better   b) another   c) harder

5. The team had a winning season, partly because of their unity.

    a) togetherness   b) team spirit   c) uniforms

LESSON III: Exercise V

Write a story using as many words from this lesson as you can. Underline the words you use.

_____

_____

_____

_____

_____

_____

_____

_____

_____

_____

_____

_____

_____

_____

_____

_____

LESSON III: Exercise VI

Circle the English derivatives in the puzzle below.

```
K I V A B U Z A N I M A L S B T N K V N
Q Z H N T H K K W O I P P X T I P G U B
I X X I O I C A T N T E Y C D N C E Q Q
N E Y M H L X B K R I N A O K C T S G M
I X Y A I G G T X R S N C U P I E G P D
T C M T D Q T F D V D S C R V T X L R Q
I I V I W A F G K E V Y U S L E C D O L
A T Z O K H N B B Z E L R E L W U M V R
L E V N Z C A D D A R V S Q A X R V O O
L M P X P P Q L O J B A I L H J S L C D
Y E P Z F R B R T J U N V F Z T I R A S
H N S A V N O H P E G I E M V U O M T U
B T V X O G P V C M R A M O G N N Q I P
E T C E T E R A O S F N T K X I U Q O E
D H Y T Y O O A Q K F O A M N S B H N R
S U P E R M A N G W E G C T Y O Z X S V
J P R D B M G P U N I T Y R E N C B B I
L X U N I V E R S I T Y T B Y E B I E S
M E E N D N R H D E Z S U P E R I O R E
O A L T E R A T I O N T Q W V Y R Q O W
```

PROVOCATION	CURSIVE	UNISON
PROVOKE	ALTERNATE	ETCETERA
ANIMALS	INCITE	EXCURSION
SUPERMAN	COURSE	EXCITEMENT
SUPERVISE	ALTERATION	INITIALLY
UNIVERSITY	SUPERIOR	PENNSYLVANIA
UNITY	ANIMATION	

29

LESSON IV: Vocabulary

Study these Latin words, their meanings, and their English derivatives.

LATIN WORD	MEANING	DERIVATIVES
1. gradus	step	degrade ingredient grade gradual retrograde graduation gradiant
2. tardus, tarda, tardum (adj)	slow	tardy to retard
3. dormīre, dormit (v)	to sleep, (he) sleeps	dormitory dormouse
4. oculī (n)	eyes	binoculars oculist ocular
5. fīnis	end	finish infinite finite confine define refine
6. maximē	very much	maximum
7. invenīre, invenit (v)	to find, (he) finds	invent invention
8. aqua (n)	water	aquatic aquarium aquamarine
9. altus, alta, altum (adj)	high	altitude exaltation altimeter
10. satis	enough	satisfy satisfactory unsatisfactory

Trace the Latin vocabulary words, meanings, and English derivatives below. Then add macrons!

1	Word & Meaning:	*gradus* *step*
	Derivatives:	*degrade, ingredient, grade, gradual, retrograde, graduation, gradiant*
2	Word & Meaning:	*tardus, tarda, tardum* *slow*
	Derivatives:	*tardy, to retard*
3	Word & Meaning:	*dormire, dormit* *to sleep, (he) sleeps*
	Derivatives:	*dormitory, dormouse*
4	Word & Meaning:	*oculi* *eyes*
	Derivatives:	*binoculars, oculist, ocular*
5	Word & Meaning:	*finis* *end*
	Derivatives:	*finish, infinite, finite, confine, define, refine*
6	Word & Meaning:	*maxime* *very much*
	Derivatives:	*maximum*
7	Word & Meaning:	*invenire, invenit* *to find, (he) finds*
	Derivatives:	*invent, invention*
8	Word & Meaning:	*aqua* *water*
	Derivatives:	*aquatic, aquarium, aquamarine*
9	Word & Meaning:	*altus, alta, altum* *high*
	Derivatives:	*altitude, exaltation, altimeter*
10	Word & Meaning:	*satis* *enough*
	Derivatives:	*satisfy, satisfactory, unsatisfactory*

LESSON IV: Exercise I

Complete the sentences using English Derivatives.

FILL IN THE BLANK

1. Did Edison_____the light bulb?

2. The homeless man ate until he was_____.

3. Because the student was_____
the teacher gave him extra work .

4. We did our work _____.

5. The fish in the_____are very
interesting.

6. The pot was filled to its_____.

7. We watched the birds with our_____.

8. The man climbed to an_____of
12,000 feet.

9. To_____well, you must work
diligently.

10. My sister lived in a_____
at college.

CHOICES

gradually

tardy

dormitory

maximum

invent

finish

satisfied

aquarium

altitude

binoculars

LESSON IV: Exercise II

Use a ruler. Draw a line to match the English derivative to its Latin word.

DERIVATIVE	LATIN WORD
1. grade, gradual	fīnis
2. tardy	oculī
3. satisfy, satisfaction	invenīre
4. altitude	gradus
5. binoculars	aqua
6. maximum	satis
7. domitory	tardus, tarda, tardum
8. finish	dormīre
9. invent	maximē
10. aquarium	altus, alta, altum

LESSON IV: Exercise III

Fill in the blanks using English derivatives. Your choices are listed at the bottom of the page.

STORY

The children in Mrs. Jenson's class went on a field trip. Thomas was

1)_____, which made the whole class wait.

The first stop was at an 2)_____ to see

the giant whales. The next place was a bird sanctuary. Most of the children brought

3)_____ so they could see the birds who hid at high

4)_____.

Everyone was 5)_____ that they had the

6)_____fun on their outing.

CHOICES

tardy   maximum   altitudes   aquarium   satisfied
binoculars

LESSON IV: Exercise IV

What does the underlined word mean? Circle your choice.

1. We looked at the birds with binoculars.

    a) sunglasses   b) a tool to see far away   c) magnifying glass

2. They did their work gradually.

    a) fast   b) step by step   c) quickly

3. Jennifer kept her pet in an old aquarium.

    a) shoe   b) doghouse   c) container (usually water-filled)

4. The maximum amount to gain is 80.

    a) lowest   b) easiest   c) highest/most

5. She left her book in the dormitory.

    a) library   b) college bedroom   c) classroom

6. What is the altitude of the mountain you climbed?

    a) height   b) width   c) temperature

LESSON IV: Exercise V

Write a story using as many words from this lesson as you can. Underline the words you use.

_____

_____

_____

_____

_____

_____

_____

_____

_____

_____

_____

_____

_____

_____

_____

_____

LESSON IV: Exercise VI

Choose <u>English derivatives</u> to solve the puzzle below. (Latin words are in parentheses).

DOWN

1) the greatest possible (maximē)
2) an instrument for viewing distant objects (oculī)
5) late (tardus, -a, -um)
6) the height of an object (altus, -a, -um)
8) to complete (fīnis)

ACROSS

3) taking place by degrees (gradus)
4) a college bedroom (dormīre)
6) a tank for keeping water creatures (aqua)
7) to meet needs and expectations (satis)
9) a process or device (invenīre)

LESSON V: Vocabulary

Study these Latin words, their meanings, and their English derivatives.

LATIN WORD	MEANING	DERIVATIVES	
1. posse, potest, poterat (v)	to be able, (he) is able, (he) was able	potential possible potent omnipotent	
2. afflictus, afflicta, afflictum (adj)	discouraged, beaten down	to afflict	
3. minimē	no way	minimum	
4. frangere, frangit (v)	to break into pieces, (he) breaks	frangible infrangible fracture fraction	infraction defract refract
5. firmus, firma, firmum (adj)	strong	firm affirm infirmary affirmation	
6. ēvertere (v)	to turn upside down	advertise subvert invert inversion divert	diversion avert aversion revert
7. gravis, gravis, grave (adj)	heavy	grave gravity engrave	
8. centum	100	cent century centipede centimeter percent	
9. relinquere, relinquit (v)	to leave behind, (he) leaves behind	relic relinquish	
10. desertum (n)	desert (wasteland)	desert (not the verb "to leave behind")	

Trace the Latin vocabulary words, meanings, and English derivatives below. Then add macrons!

1	Word & Meaning:	posse, potest, poterat
		to be able, (he) is able, (he) was able
	Derivatives:	potential, possible, potent, omnipotent
2	Word & Meaning:	afflictus, afflicta, afflictum discouraged, beaten down
	Derivatives:	to afflict
3	Word & Meaning:	minime no way
	Derivatives:	minimum
4	Word & Meaning:	frangere, frangit
		to break into pieces, (he) breaks into pieces
	Derivatives:	frangible, infrangible, fracture, fraction, infraction,
		defract, refract
5	Word & Meaning:	firmus, firma, firmum strong
	Derivatives:	firm, affirm, infirmary, affirmation
6	Word & Meaning:	evertere to turn upside down
	Derivatives:	advertise, subvert, invert, inversion, divert, diversion
		avert, aversion, revert
7	Word & Meaning:	gravis, gravis, grave heavy
	Derivatives:	grave, gravity, engrave
8	Word & Meaning:	centum 100, hundred
	Derivatives:	cent, century, centipede, centimeter, percent
9	Word & Meaning:	relinquere, relinquit
		to leave behind, (he) leaves behind
	Derivatives:	relic, relinquish
10	Word & Meaning:	desertum desert (wasteland)
	Derivatives:	desert

LESSON V: Exercise I

Complete the sentences using English Derivatives.

FILL IN THE BLANK

CHOICES

1. Tommy had to_____the jar to get the marbles.

gravity

relinquish

2. She had the _____ to become a famous pianist.

fraction

3. It was so hot in the _____we drank all our water.

cents

potential

4. If God had not made_____, we would float off the ground.

invert

5. With only a_____of effort, we won the contest.

minimum

6. Papa Bear said, "This bed is too_____."

firm

7. This dime is equal to ten_____.

desert

8. We were tired, but had only done a_____ of our work.

9. They wanted us to_____ our rights. We said, "No."

40

LESSON V: Exercise II

Use a ruler. Draw a line to match the English derivative to its Latin word.

DERIVATIVE	LATIN WORD
1. to afflict	gravis, gravis, grave
2. firm	minimē
3. potential	fīrmus, fīrma, fīrmum
4. gravity	afflictus, afflicta, afflictum
5. fraction, fracture	centum
6. relic, relinquish (to give up something)	posse, potest, poterat
7. century, percent, cent	ēvertere
8. minimum	frangere
9. advertise, invert, divert, revert	desertum
10. desert (n., wasteland)	relinquit

LESSON V: Exercise III

Fill in the blanks using English derivatives. Your choices are listed at the bottom of the page.

STORY

In an earlier 1)_____, scientists did not

understand 2)_____. A small

3)_____ of them realized how important this was.

They placed an 4)_____ in a magazine called

"Gravity at Work." They asked for a 5)_____ of

ten fellow students to join them in their study of gravity.

They were 6)_____ that scientists must

7)_____ old ideas and make progress into the 20th

8) _____.

CHOICES

firm	relinquish	gravity	minimum	century
century	fraction	advertisement		

42

LESSON V: Exercise IV

What does the underlined word mean? Circle your choice.

1. When the pickle jar was <u>inverted</u>, the pickles floated to the top.

   a) broken   b) turned upside down   c) shaken

2. Her leg had two <u>fractures</u>.

   a) breaks   b) marks   c) bites

3. The salesman asked, "What <u>percent</u> are you willing to pay?"

   a) amount   b) dollars   c) portion

4. The apple was <u>firm</u>, so we knew it was ripe.

   a) musty   b) red   c) solid

5. The student has the <u>potential</u> to go to college.

   a) strong possibility   b) inability   c) desire

43

LESSON V: Exercise V

Write a story using as many words from this lesson as you can. Underline the words you use.

_____

_____

_____

_____

_____

_____

_____

_____

_____

_____

_____

_____

_____

_____

_____

_____

LESSON V: Exercise VI

Circle the English derivatives in the puzzle below.

```
R  Y  M  I  N  I  M  U  M  N  G  E  N  G  R  A  V  E  P  T
K  F  P  T  S  P  A  E  V  A  S  T  Z  T  W  E  V  F  O  Z
A  F  F  I  R  M  A  T  I  O  N  B  Z  G  P  O  P  R  T  J
E  A  P  N  W  L  F  Q  X  U  I  L  M  R  S  C  G  A  E  L
X  R  V  H  M  G  V  T  I  G  X  J  N  Z  B  R  K  C  N  A
P  U  P  E  M  D  I  R  L  D  B  Q  H  L  L  F  A  T  T  P
W  L  E  I  R  O  E  N  E  K  P  H  L  X  F  S  H  U  I  E
C  P  L  D  E  S  M  S  V  L  U  H  K  V  R  F  U  R  A  R
O  S  K  V  P  B  I  N  E  E  I  R  C  V  E  L  Q  E  L  C
C  F  R  A  C  T  I  O  N  R  R  C  E  E  L  U  L  Z  O  E
G  E  G  S  B  X  P  U  N  M  T  T  N  D  I  J  Q  B  M  N
W  R  N  A  M  X  V  G  P  T  H  Z  D  N  Y  A  R  N  T
M  W  A  T  O  A  F  F  L  I  C  T  U  N  Q  A  T  L  I  E
U  B  M  V  I  G  N  P  M  H  T  H  R  V  U  Y  V  Q  P  F
O  W  M  K  I  P  N  U  L  V  Z  K  Y  F  I  H  K  R  O  Y
P  B  W  I  A  T  E  S  Y  I  I  U  Y  X  S  M  A  K  T  M
I  J  G  T  L  N  Y  D  D  U  G  O  D  A  H  I  Y  K  E  O
O  C  Q  Y  H  F  O  V  E  J  H  K  T  B  B  Q  Y  R  N  Z
R  E  F  R  A  C  T  G  A  D  V  E  R  T  I  S  E  N  T  E
A  D  Y  C  E  N  V  A  B  F  I  R  M  A  N  U  P  K  L  A
```

RELINQUISH	RELIC	AVERSION
REFRACT	PERCENT	GRAVITY
FIRM	AFFIRMATION	CENTIPEDE
FRACTURE	DESERT	MINIMUM
FRACTION	AFFLICT	ADVERTISE
OMNIPOTENT	POTENTIAL	CENTURY
ENGRAVE	INVERT	

REVIEW: Part I

Write one English derivative for each Latin word from Lessons I - V.

LATIN WORD	DERIVATIVE	LATIN WORD	DERIVATIVE
1. portāre	_____	11. ūnus, ūna, ūnum	_____
2. initium	_____	12. prīmus, -a, -um	_____
3. altus, -a, -um	_____	13. porcus	_____
4. posse, potest	_____	14. māter	_____
5. trēs, trēs, tria	_____	15. alter, -a, -um	_____
6. gradus	_____	16. aqua	_____
7. audīre	_____	17. respondēre	_____
8. fīnis	_____	18. currere	_____
9. gravis, -is, -e	_____	19. dicere, dīcit	_____
10. frangere	_____	20. firmus, -a, -um	_____

REVIEW: Part II

Write ten sentences using the derivatives you listed on Page 46.

1. _____

_____

2. _____

_____

3. _____

_____

4. _____

_____

5. _____

_____

6. _____

_____

7. _____

_____

8. _____

_____

9. _____

_____

10. _____

_____

LESSON VI: Vocabulary

Study these Latin words, their meanings, and their English derivatives.

Latin Word	Meaning	Derivatives	
1. impōnere, impōnō, impōnit (v)	to place (on) I place (on), (he) places (on)	postpone impose depose oppose opponent proponent component	compose propose suppose interpose transpose position
2. domus (n)	home	domesticated dominion superdome	dome dominant dominate
3. formīca (n)	ant	formica	
4. lūdere, lūdit (v)	to play, (he) plays	allude allusion prelude elude ludicrous	delude deluded interlude ridiculous delusion
5. sōl (n)	sunshine	solarium solar	
6. quaerere, quaerit (v)	to look for, (he) looks for	acquire inquire prerequisite	require question
7. mōtus (n)	the motion	motion motive motor remote	demote demotion promotion move
8. vīvus, vīvā, vīvum (adj)	alive	vivacious vivid vivisection	revive revival
9. ego (n)	I	egotist ego	egomaniac egocentric
10. captīvus (n)	captive	capture captive	captivate caption

		Trace the Latin vocabulary words, meanings, and English derivatives below. Then add macrons!
1	Word & Meaning:	imponere, impono, imponit to place (on), I place (on), (he) places (on)
	Derivatives:	postpone, impose, depose, oppose, opponent, proponent, component, compose, propose, suppose, interpose, transpose, position
2	Word & Meaning:	domus home
	Derivatives:	domesticated, dominion, superdome, dome, dominant, dominate
3	Word & Meaning:	formica ant
	Derivatives:	formica
4	Word & Meaning:	ludere, ludit to play, (he) plays
	Derivatives:	allude, allusion, prelude, elude, ludicrous, delude, deluded interlude, ridiculous, delusion
5	Word & Meaning:	sol sunshine
	Derivatives:	solarium, solar
6	Word & Meaning:	quaerere, quaerit to look for, (he) looks for
	Derivatives:	acquire, inquire, require, prerequisite, question
7	Word & Meaning:	motus the motion
	Derivatives:	motion, motive, motor, remote, demote, demotion, promotion, move
8	Word & Meaning:	vivus, viva, vivum alive
	Derivatives:	vivacious, vivid, vivisection, revive, revival
9	Word & Meaning:	ego I
	Derivatives:	egotist, ego, egomaniac, egocentric
10	Word & Meaning:	captivus captive
	Derivatives:	capture, captive, captivate, caption

LESSON VI: Exercise I

Complete the sentences using English Derivatives.

FILL IN THE BLANK   CHOICES

1. The kitchen had_____   inquire
countertops.

                                                                  dome
2. The _____ of the swimmer's arms
was perfect.

                                                                  formica

3. She will_____ in the bank about
her question.
                                                                  capture

4. The_____only thought of himself.
                                                                  solar

5. If the hunter is careful, he can _____
the lion.   egotist

6. The boy was so_____, the others   motion
couldn't keep up with him.

                                                                  vivacious

7. The children decided not to _____
on the elderly man.
                                                                  impose

8. The boy made a_____suggestion.

                                                                  ludicrous

9. We installed several_____ panels
on the roof.

10. The old church has a_____for a roof.

LESSON VI: Exercise II

Use a ruler. Draw a line to match the English derivative to its Latin word.

DERIVATIVE	LATIN WORD
1. acquire, inquire	captīvus
2. motion	impōnere
3. impose	formīca
4. domesticated, dome, dominate	sōl
5. solar	quaerere, quaerit
6. capture	mōtus
7. formica	ego
8. vivacious	lūdere, lūdit
9. egotist	domus
10. elude, ludicrous	vīvus, vīvā, vīvum

LESSON VI: Exercise III

Fill in the blanks using English derivatives. Your choices are listed at the bottom of the page.

STORY

The hunting expedition left for Africa on Monday. The hunting party took

lots of equipment. They even took some 1)_____ -

powered flashlights. They didn't want anything to 2)_____

the hunt, not even darkness.

For a short time, they were lost, but they stopped to

3)_____ which way to go. Unfortunately, the

leader of the group was an 4)_____ and thought he

knew everything. He even thought he could 5)_____

a lion as if it were a 6)_____ cat.

_____

CHOICES

egomaniac   domesticated   postpone   solar   inquire   capture

LESSON VI: Exercise IV

What does the underlined word mean? Circle your choice.

1. The child's behavior was so <u>ludicrous</u>, the others were shocked.

    a) delightful   b) ridiculous   c) sad

2. We will <u>inquire</u> which way to go.

    a) ask   b) decide   c) be confused about

3. The <u>motion</u> of the ship made us sick.

    a) rocking   b) smell   c) movement

4. They gathered electricity from the <u>solar</u> panels.

    a) moon   b) sun   c) stars

5. Because the animal had been <u>domesticated</u>, we were able to have it as a pet.

    a) barn trained   b) house trained   c) groomed

6. The pupil was such an <u>egotist</u>, no one wanted to play with him.

    a) kind person   b) good player   c) selfish person

LESSON VI: Exercise V

Write a story using as many words from this lesson as you can. Underline the words you use.

_____

_____

_____

_____

_____

_____

_____

_____

_____

_____

_____

_____

_____

_____

_____

_____

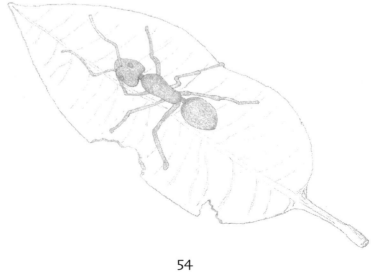

LESSON VI: Exercise VI

Choose <u>English derivatives</u> to solve the puzzle below. (Latin words are in parentheses.)

DOWN

1) tame and kept as a pet (domus)
2) something required for something else to happen or exist (quaerere)
3) to write (a poem or song) (impōnere)
5) a prisoner (captīvus)
6) a hard plastic used for countertops (formīca)

ACROSS

4) energy from the sun (sōl)
7) a reason for doing something (mōtus)
8) a selfish person (ego)
9) a piece of music played between other pieces (lūdere)
10) lively and animated (vīvus, vīvā, vīvum)

LESSON VII: Vocabulary

Study these Latin words, their meanings, and their English derivatives.

Latin Word	Meaning	Derivatives
1. carcer (n)	prison	incarcerate
2. cauda (n)	tail	coda (end of a musical piece)
3. vacuus, vacua, vacuum (adj)	empty	vacant vacuum vacuous vacation
4. umbra (n)	shadow	umbrella umbrage penumbra sombrero
5. appārēre, appāret (v)	to appear, (he) appears	apparition disappear appear
6. suspicere, suspicit (v)	to look up, (he) looks up	suspicion suspect
7. clāmāre, clāmat (v)	to shout, (he) shouts	clamor exclamatory reclaim exclaim acclaim proclaim
8. volāre, volat (v)	to fly, (he) flies	volatile
9. sōlus, sōla, sōlum (adj)	only	sole solitary solitaire desolation
10. homō (n)	man, person	homicide hominid

Trace the Latin vocabulary words, meanings, and English derivatives below. Then add macrons!

1	Word & Meaning:	carcer	prison
	Derivatives:	incarcerate	
2	Word & Meaning:	cauda	tail
	Derivatives:	coda	
3	Word & Meaning:	vacuus, vacua, vacuum	empty
	Derivatives:	vacant, vacuum, vacuous, vacation	
4	Word & Meaning:	umbra	shadow
	Derivatives:	umbrella, umbrage, penumbra, sombrero	
5	Word & Meaning:	apparere, apparet	to appear, (he) appears
	Derivatives:	apparition, disappear, appear	
6	Word & Meaning:	suspicere, suspicit	to look up, (he) looks up
	Derivatives:	suspicion, suspect	
7	Word & Meaning:	clamare, clamat	to shout, (he) shouts
	Derivatives:	clamor, exclamatory, reclaim, exclaim, acclaim, proclaim	
8	Word & Meaning:	volare, volat	to fly, (he) flies
	Derivatives:	volatile	
9	Word & Meaning:	solus, sola, solum	only
	Derivatives:	sole, solitary, solitaire, desolation	
10	Word & Meaning:	homo	man, person
	Derivatives:	homicide, hominid	

LESSON VII: Exercise I

Complete the sentences using English Derivatives.

FILL IN THE BLANK   CHOICES

1. We went to the beach for our_____.   vacant

2. The girl made sure she took her_____   solitary
in case of storms.

                                                                        suspect
3. She got a speeding ticket, so she will have to

_____ before the judge.   vacation

4. In the library, you shouldn't make a
                                                                        appear
_____sound.

5. After tearing down the building, there was just a

_____ lot.   incarcerated

6. Many detective stories are about_____.   umbrella

7. When the ring was stolen, the police had a
                                                                        clamor

_____.

                                                                        homocides
8. The thief was found and was_____.

                                                                        volatile
9. Because he has a nasty temper and flies off the handle, we says

he is_____.

10. In "The Night Before Christmas," it says, "When up on the

roof, there arose such a _____."

LESSON VII: Exercise II

Use a ruler. Draw a line to match the English derivative to its Latin word.

DERIVATIVE	LATIN WORD
1. incarcerate	homō
2. clamor	vacuua, vacua, vacuum
3. sole, solitary, solitaire, desolation	volāre
4. apparition, appear	umbra
5. homicide	sōlus, sōla, sōlum
6. coda	carcer
7. umbrella	suspicere
8. vacant, vacation	clāmāre
9. suspicion	cauda
10. volatile	appārēre

LESSON VII: Exercise III

Fill in the blanks using English derivatives. Your choices are listed at the bottom of the page.

STORY

The newspaper reported that a man had died.

They call it a 1)_____ when there is a

2)_____ of foul play. He had been found in a

3)_____ lot. A passerby 4)_____,

"Get help!"

The police found their suspect. He 5)_____

before a judge and was found guilty. Then he was 6)_____.

He wasn't sorry and did not cry a 7)_____ tear.

_____

CHOICES

incarcerated	appeared	homocide	solitary	vacant
suspicion	exclaimed			

LESSON VII: Exercise IV

What does the underlined word mean? Circle your choice.

1. That song has a beautiful <u>coda</u>.

    a) ending   b) chord   c) music

2. The <u>clamor</u> was so disturbing we could not hear the teacher.

    a) musician   b) clown   c) shouting

3. Susan was the <u>sole</u> winner.

    a) happy   b) only   c) first

4. The lost puppy was found in a <u>vacant</u> building.

    a) violet   b) empty   c) messy

5. The <u>apparition</u> turned out to be an angel.

    a) girl   b) appearance   c) noise

LESSON VII: Exercise V

Write a story using as many words from this lesson as you can. Underline the words you use.

_____

_____

_____

_____

_____

_____

_____

_____

_____

_____

_____

_____

_____

_____

LESSON VII: Exercise VI

Circle the English derivatives in the puzzle below.

```
Y  N  M  N  G  W  P  Q  Y  I  T  Y  P  U  Y  F  C  L  H  N
C  E  X  C  L  A  M  A  T  O  R  Y  I  M  J  M  W  C  Z  H
M  I  H  O  M  I  N  I  D  E  C  E  N  B  D  J  O  P  V  K
E  I  D  F  H  T  K  H  V  Y  U  Q  C  R  S  V  N  N  D  C
V  A  C  U  U  M  E  A  X  H  A  G  A  A  O  O  G  W  X  V
H  K  O  O  W  Y  P  D  B  I  S  K  R  G  M  L  F  Z  S  A
O  A  R  T  L  L  O  S  O  I  H  C  C  E  B  A  H  J  U  C
M  D  V  C  L  A  M  O  R  B  Y  Y  E  P  R  T  G  S  S  A
I  E  C  W  S  F  G  I  K  D  C  J  R  F  E  I  M  O  P  T
C  S  L  D  R  B  A  W  C  L  N  F  A  C  R  L  B  L  I  I
I  O  V  H  I  D  Q  J  Z  V  O  N  T  D  O  E  N  I  C  O
D  L  H  M  N  S  Y  U  S  S  V  U  E  T  E  G  N  T  I  N
E  A  O  X  Z  T  A  T  S  U  E  X  M  Z  D  F  R  A  O  A
O  T  M  H  O  A  R  P  S  S  P  N  B  B  C  X  W  R  N  W
J  I  P  A  G  I  V  T  P  P  E  P  I  M  R  D  B  Y  L  K
S  O  O  R  U  L  M  N  E  E  H  V  F  Z  I  E  U  Z  R  C
K  N  Q  M  A  A  T  H  E  C  A  X  S  I  J  V  L  Y  P  O
S  W  V  A  C  A  N  T  M  T  P  R  I  S  S  F  V  L  Z  D
Z  K  I  H  E  X  C  L  A  I  M  X  F  L  H  X  W  K  A  A
V  V  A  P  P  A  R  I  T  I  O  N  U  E  Q  W  W  A  O  S
```

UMBRAGE	SOMBRERO	CODA
VACUUM	HOMINID	UMBRELLA
HOMICIDE	INCARCERATE	SUSPECT
DISAPPEAR	VACANT	EXCLAIM
DESOLATION	VACATION	CLAMOR
SUSPICION	EXCLAMATORY	SOLITARY
APPARITION	VOLATILE	

LESSON VIII: Vocabulary

Study these Latin words, their meanings, and their English derivatives.

LATIN WORD	MEANING	DERIVATIVES
1. discendere, dēscendit	to come down, (he) comes down	descend ascend transcend descendants
2. nomināre	to name	nominate
3. verberāre, verberat	to beat, (he) beats	reverberate
4. sacerdōs	priest	sacred sacrifice sacrament
5. ambulāre, ambulat	to walk, (he) walks	amble ambulance perambulator
6. via	road	viaduct via obvious deviate
7. cōnsistere	to stop	consistent consist
8. dare, dat, dedit	to give, (he) gives, (he) gave	dedicate
9. auxilium	help	auxiliary
10. obscura	dark, hidden	obscured unobscured

Trace the Latin vocabulary words, meanings, and English derivatives below. Then add macrons!

1	Word & Meaning:	discendere, descendit to come down, (he) comes down
	Derivatives:	descend, ascend, transcend, descendants
2	Word & Meaning:	nominare to name
	Derivatives:	nominate
3	Word & Meaning:	verberare, verberat to beat, (he) beats
	Derivatives:	reverberate
4	Word & Meaning:	sacerdos priest
	Derivatives:	sacred, sacrifice, sacrament
5	Word & Meaning:	ambulare, ambulat to walk, (he) walks
	Derivatives:	amble, ambulance, perambulator
6	Word & Meaning:	via road
	Derivatives:	viaduct, via, obvious, deviate
7	Word & Meaning:	consistere to stop
	Derivatives:	consistent, consist
8	Word & Meaning:	dare, dat, dedit to give, (he) gives, (he) gave
	Derivatives:	dedicate
9	Word & Meaning:	auxilium help
	Derivatives:	auxiliary
10	Word & Meaning:	obscura dark, hidden
	Derivatives:	obscured, unobscured

LESSON VIII: Exercise I

Complete the sentences using English Derivatives.

FILL IN THE BLANK   CHOICES

1. The firefighter climbed out of the window and   via

_____the ladder.

               consistently

2. The boy_____his brother for an
award.

               descended

3. Christians believe Jesus is a_____
in their place.

               nominated

4. The drum_____ in our ears.

               obscured

5. We talked to our grandchildren_____the phone.

               sacrifice

6. If you study_____ , you will do
well.

               dedicated

7. They took the injured woman to the hospital in an

_____.

               reverberated

8. The ladies_____group helped the
hospital.

               auxiliary

               ambulance

9. Because of the fog, the road was_____.

10. The author_____her book to her
son.

LESSON VIII: Exercise II

Use a ruler. Draw a line to match the English derivative to its Latin word.

DERIVATIVE	LATIN WORD
1. sacred, sacrifice	ambulāre, ambulābat
2. via (by way of), deviate	nomināre
3. obscured, unobscured	via
4. descend	obscura
5. dedicate	sacerdōs
6. amble, ambulance	dēscendere
7. nominate	verberāre
8. consistent	dare, dat, dedit
9. auxiliary	auxilium
10. reverberate	cōnsistere

LESSON VIII: Exercise III

Fill in the blanks using English derivatives. Your choices are listed at the bottom of the page.

STORY

The boy's group went on a mountain hike. The plan was to

1)_____ the long way, because it was less

strenuous. They agreed not to 2) _____ from the plan

unless necessary. Though they were 3)_____with the plan,

nature got in the way. Part of the way up, the path was blocked with huge boulders.

They picked an 4)_____route. Doing this forced them

to 5)_____ instead of continuing their upward climb. It was

fortunate, though, because just then the mountain began to

6)_____. Rocks fell everywhere, but they were able to

reach safety just in time.

CHOICES

obscure   descend   ascend   consistent   deviate   reverberate

LESSON VIII: Exercise IV

What does the underlined word mean? Circle your choice.

1. The <u>sacred</u> book was put in a special place for safekeeping.

      a) very old   b) large   c) holy

2. In the evening, we will <u>amble</u> through the countryside.

      a) walk   b) run   c) race

3. We are going to leave quickly <u>via</u> the tunnel.

      a) unfortunately   b) by way of   c) over

4. The sound <u>reverberated</u> through the walls.

      a) echoed   b) whispered   c) dripped

5. The author <u>dedicated</u> her book to her only son.

      a) gave honor in   b) sent   c) illustrated

6. We were surprised how fast the rain <u>descended</u>.

      a) evaporated   b) collected   c) fell

LESSON VIII: Exercise V

Write a story using as many words from this lesson as you can. Underline the words you use.

_____

_____

_____

_____

_____

_____

_____

_____

_____

_____

_____

_____

_____

_____

_____

LESSON VIII: Exercise VI

Choose <u>English derivatives</u> to solve the puzzle below. (Latin words are in parentheses.)

DOWN

3) a baby carriage (ambulāre)
5) unchanging (consistere)
6) extra help (auxilium)
8) holy (sacerdōs)
10) to repeat a sound as an echo (verberāre)

ACROSS

1) waterway (viā)
2) devote to a task or purpose (dare)
4) to propose or appoint
7) to walk at a relaxed pace (ambulāre)
9) move or fall downward (dīscendere)

LESSON IX: Vocabulary

Study these Latin words, their meanings, and their English derivatives.

LATIN WORD	MEANING	DERIVATIVES	
1. prope	near	approach propinquity	
2. vulnus, vulnera (n)	wound, wounds	vulnerable invulnerable	
3. īnfūdere, infūsit (v)	to pour (over), (he) poured (over)	infuse infusion fuse fusion confuse	suffuse profuse defuse refuse
4. oleum (n)	oil	oil	
5. vīnum (n)	wine	wine vine vintner	
6. noctem (n)	night	nocturnal	
7. dūcere, dūcit, dūxit (v)	to lead, (he) leads, (he) led	conductor reduce induce produce deduce introduce conductive	
8. stabulum n)	stable	stable	
9. cūrāre, cūrat, cūrāvit (v)	to take care of, (he) takes care of (he) took care of	curator procure	
10. proximus, proxima, proximum (adj)	next	approximate proximity	

\multicolumn{4}{l}{Trace the Latin vocabulary words, meanings, and English derivatives below. Then add macrons!}

1	Word & Meaning:	prope	near
	Derivatives:	approach, propinquity	
2	Word & Meaning:	vulnus, vulnera	wound, wounds
	Derivatives:	vulnerable, invulnerable	
3	Word & Meaning:	infudere, infusit	
		to pour (over), (he) poured (over)	
	Derivatives:	infuse, infusion, fuse, fusion, confuse, suffuse, profuse,	
		defuse, refuse	
4	Word & Meaning:	oleum	oil
	Derivatives:	oil	
5	Word & Meaning:	vinum	wine
	Derivatives:	wine, vine, vintner	
6	Word & Meaning:	noctem	night
	Derivatives:	nocturnal	
7	Word & Meaning:	ducere, ducit, duxit	to lead, (he) leads, (he) led
	Derivatives:	conductor, reduce, induce, produce, deduce, introduce	
		conductive	
8	Word & Meaning:	stabulum	stable
	Derivatives:	stable	
9	Word & Meaning:	curare, curat, curavit	
		to take care of, (he) takes care of, (he) took care of	
	Derivatives:	curator, procure	
10	Word & Meaning:	proximus, proxima, proximum next	
	Derivatives:	approximate, proximity	

LESSON IX: Exercise I

Complete the sentences using English Derivatives.

FILL IN THE BLANK	CHOICES

1. The boys changed the_____ in the car.

approximately

2. If you gently strum the strings on a guitar, it will

_____ a nice sound.

vine

3. When the car_____the gate, the
driver paid the toll.

oil

wine

4. The time was_____ 3:15.

approached

5. Grapes grow on a_____.

produce

6. Grapes can be used to make grape juice or_____.

vulnerable

7. The donkey and the cow sleep together in the

_____.

nocturnal

stable

8. The _____of the museum let us in.

curator

9. The girl felt _____because she was
alone.

10. Because the owl is a _____ creature, we
had to stay up very late to see it.

LESSON IX: Exercise II

Use a ruler. Draw a line to match the English derivative to its Latin word.

DERIVATIVE	LATIN WORD
1. infuse, infusion	prope
2. wine, vine	vulnus
3. conductor, reduce, induce	īnfūdere
4. approach	oleum
5. vulnerable, invulnerable	vīnum
6. approximate	noctem
7. oil	dūcere, dūxit
8. nocturnal	stabulum
9. stable	cūrāre
10. curator	proximus, proxima, proximum

LESSON IX: Exercise III

Fill in the blanks using English derivatives. Your choices are listed at the bottom of the page.

STORY

The train was moving at 1)_____ 250 miles

per hour. As it went around the curve, it jumped the tracks and raced across the field.

As it 2)_____ a 3)_____,

animals ran out of the way. It finally came to a stop. Though everyone felt

4) _____, no one was seriously hurt. The

5)_____ went through the train checking all wounds.

He poured medicinal 6)_____ on each wound he found. All

were glad when things calmed down.

_____

CHOICES

conductor   oil   approximately   vulnerable   approached   stable

LESSON IX: Exercise IV

What does the underlined word mean? Circle your choice.

1. In order to <u>reduce</u> costs, the ownwer stopped giving away coupons.

    a) change   b) raise   c) lower

2. The price of the two shirts was <u>approximately</u> the same.

    a) nearly   b) not at all   c) exactly

3. The <u>curator</u> of the museum refused to let the ruffians enter.

    a) caretaker   b) janitor   c) owner

4. As they <u>approached</u> the store, they were surprised to see that it was closed.

    a) opened   b) drew near   c) called

5. Can I <u>induce</u> you to take a taste?

    a) persuade   b) force   c)trap

6. Which of these would drive the train?

    a) curator   b) conductor   c) shopkeeper

LESSON IX: Exercise V

Write a story using as many words from this lesson as you can. Underline the words you use.

_____

_____

_____

_____

_____

_____

_____

_____

_____

_____

_____

_____

_____

_____

_____

LESSON IX: Exercise VI

Circle the English derivatives in the puzzle below.

```
C R W U G O F L R U P N C G O W I N E W
O C A P P R O A C H I O K M Q P P O P P
N M P R O X I M I T Y N C J S Y P I R F
F A Q X V K X A A K Q J T S T Q M E O C
U P H W I N F U S I O N Y R K D J I D U
S U V K M Y S M O P W W R N O D S W U R
E O U A A P M A O A O O Y V W D N K C A
O H L P X A S K V F N U U C D K U K E T
X K N P L A Z N R F O V J I Y Q G C G O
M S E R S C O N D U C T O R M L V O E R
J Z R O S T M I N F T S U F F U S E V F
Q I A X G Y A R U M U K J L X R E S P U
V Q B I U V Z B K P R F Y I P G G T F S
I J L M K A U K L X N M G U S Y L T P E
N A E A X F N E C E A Z T Z U J X V T D
T L R T J K H L S X L P F W O Q C Y K O
N G S E N Z Z S N R U P X H R C H N W N
E B P F E Z Y V C O N D U C T I V E R Q
R O C X O I L O O F Q N K X C W K Q G E
P R O C U R E D P R O P I N Q U I T Y M
```

PROPINQUITY	CONDUCTOR	OIL
CONFUSE	WINE	PROCURE
NOCTURNAL	VULNERABLE	INTRODUCE
INFUSION	VINTNER	CURATOR
SUFFUSE	CONDUCTIVE	APPROACH
FUSE	STABLE	APPROXIMATE
PRODUCE	PROXIMITY	

LESSON X: Vocabulary

Study these Latin words, their meanings, and their English derivatives.

LATIN WORD	MEANING	DERIVATIVES	
1. leō (n)	lion	Leo (zodiac sign) leonine	
2. pēs, pedēs (n)	paw/foot, paws/feet	pedal pedestrian pedestal	impede expedition expedite
3. aperīre, aperit, aperuit (v)	to open, (he) opens, (he) opened	April (when flowers open) aperture	
4. edere, edit (v)	to eat, (he) eats	edible inedible	
5. rēx (n) regere (n)	king to rule	regal reign region regular	regulation irregular regime regicide
6. beneficium (n)	a favor, a good deed	benefactor benificence beneficial	
7. līber, lībera, līberum (adj)	free, released	liberty libertine liberate liberal	
8. capere, capit, cēpit (v)	to catch/seize, (he) catches, (he) caught	capture caption captive concept perceive perception interception	deceive deception accept inception exception receive reception
9. ligare, ligat, ligāvit (v)	to tie, (he) ties, (he) tied	ligament ligation ligature	oblige obligation
10. lustrāre	to shine light on	illustrate illustration	

Trace the Latin vocabulary words, meanings, and English derivatives below. Then add macrons!

| 1 | Word & Meaning: | leo   lion |
| | Derivatives: | Leo, leonine |

| 2 | Word & Meaning: | pes, pedes   paw/foot, paws/feet |
| | Derivatives: | pedal, pedestrian, pedestal, impede, expedition, expedite |

3	Word & Meaning:	aperire, aperit, aperuit
		to open, (he) opens, (he) opened
	Derivatives:	April, aperture

| 4 | Word & Meaning: | edere, edit   to eat, (he) eats |
| | Derivatives: | edible, inedible |

| 5 | Word & Meaning: | rex, regere   king, to rule |
| | Derivatives: | regal, reign, region, regular, regulation, irregular, regime, regicide |

| 6 | Word & Meaning: | beneficium   a favor, a good deed |
| | Derivatives: | benefactor, benificence, beneficial |

| 7 | Word & Meaning: | liber, libera, liberum   free, released |
| | Derivatives: | liberty, libertine, liberate, liberal |

8	Word & Meaning:	capere, capit, cepit
		to catch/seize, (he) catches, (he) caught
	Derivatives:	capture, caption, captive, concept, perceive, perception, interception, deceive, deception, accept, inception, exception, receive, reception

| 9 | Word & Meaning: | ligare, ligat, ligavit   to tie, (he) ties, (he) tied |
| | Derivatives: | ligament, ligation, ligature, oblige, obligation |

| 10 | Word & Meaning: | lustrare   to shine light on |
| | Derivatives: | illustrate, illustration |

LESSON X: Exercise I

Complete the sentences using English Derivatives.

FILL IN THE BLANK   CHOICES

1. His_____ took care of all his expenses.   pedestrian

2. The zoo had many animals, including a large_____.   April

3. The driver was careful not to hit the_____   Leo

4. We receive much rain in_____.   benefactor

5. There is a constellation called_____.   ligament

6. We checked the food to see if it was_____.   lion

7. King James_____for many years.   captive

8. We should treasure our_____; it
did not come easily.   reigned

9. The prisoner was held_____.   edible

10. He tore the _____in his leg.   liberty

LESSON X: Exercise II

Use a ruler. Draw a line to match the English derivative to its Latin word.

DERIVATIVE   LATIN WORD

1. illustrate   pēs, pedēs

2. edible   edere

3. benefactor   ligāre

4. Leo   līber, -a, -um

5. pedal, pedestrian, pedestal   lustrāre

6. ligament   capere

7. regal, reign   aperīre

8. April   leō

9. liberty, liberate, liberal   rēx, regere

10. capture, accept, captive   beneficium

LESSON X: Exercise III

Fill in the blanks using English derivatives. Your choices are listed at the bottom of the page.

STORY

The month was 1)_____. The time had

finally arrived. The men who had been 2)_____were now

to be 3)_____. Though they had been fortunate to

have a 4)_____ , the food they had received was

barely 5)_____. They were told, "Be ready so

that when the door opens, you can leave." As the door opened, the look on their faces

6)_____great joy. When they got out, they were

given bread, cheese, milk, and more! Though it was simple food, they felt like

7)_____ .

CHOICES

edible   royalty   April   benefactor   captured   liberated
illustrated

84

LESSON X: Exercise IV

What does the underlined word mean? Circle your choice.

1. The <u>pedestrian</u> was not obeying the traffic signs.

    a) driver   b) cyclist   c) walking person

2. If the food is not <u>edible</u>, throw it out.

    a) able to be eaten   b) cold   c) cooked

3. He shall <u>reign</u> forever.

    a) rule   b) eat   c) be happy

4. They were grateful to their <u>benefactor</u>.

    a) buddy   b) giver of gifts   c) brother

5. With <u>liberty</u> comes responsibility.

    a) freedom   b) fun   c) learning

6. A torn <u>ligament</u> is very painful.

    a) lining   b) connective tissue   c) fingernail

LESSON X: Exercise V

Write a story using as many words from this lesson as you can. Underline the words you use.

_____

_____

_____

_____

_____

_____

_____

_____

_____

_____

_____

_____

_____

_____

LESSON X: Exercise VI

Choose <u>English derivatives</u> to solve the puzzle below. (Latin words are in parentheses.)

DOWN

1) a journey (pēs)
2) a foot-operated level (pēs)
4) a person who gives money to a cause (beneficium)
5) resembling a lion (leō)
7) tissue that attaches bones (ligāre)

ACROSS

3) able to be eaten (edere)
6) magnificent and dignified (rēx)
8) freedom (līber, lībera, līberum)
9) the fourth month (aperīre)
10) to lead astray (capere)

REVIEW: Part I

Write one English derivative for each Latin word from Lessons VI-X. (Multiple possible answers!)

LATIN WORD	DERIVATIVE	LATIN WORD	DERIVATIVE
1. lūdere	_____	11. verberāre	_____
2. vacuus, -a, -um	_____	12, vīvus, -a, -um	_____
3. via	_____	13. īnfūdere	_____
4. proximus, -a, -um	_____	14. quaerere	_____
5. domus	_____	15. carcer	_____
6. volāre	_____	16. sōlus, -a, -um	_____
7. alter, -a, -um	_____	17. sacerdōs	_____
8. rēx, regere	_____	18. vulnus	_____
9. pēs	_____	19. dūcere	_____
10. līber, -a, -um	_____	20. edere	_____

REVIEW: Part II

Write ten sentences using the derivatives you listed on Page 88.

1. _____

_____

2. _____

_____

3. _____

_____

4. _____

_____

5. _____

_____

6. _____

_____

7. _____

_____

8. _____

_____

9. _____

_____

10. _____

_____

LESSON XI: Vocabulary

Study these Latin words, their meanings, and their English derivatives.

LATIN WORD	MEANING	DERIVATIVES	
1. vehiculum (n)	wagon, carriage	vehicle vehicular	invection
2. rōdere, rōdit, rōsit (v)	to gnaw, (he) gnaws, (he) gnawed	erode rodent	corrode corrosion
3. circum	around	circumference circle circus circumnavigate	circular circa circulation
4. certē	indeed, certainly	certainly certain	uncertain ascertain
5. diēs (n)	day	diary diurnal journal sundial	per diem antemeridian postmeridian
6. trānsīre, trānsit, trānsiit (v)	to cross, (he) crosses, (he) crossed	transition transit transpose transmit	transmission traitor translate
7. mare (n)	sea	marine maritime submarine	aquamarine mare (moon sea)
8. turba (n)	crowd	disturb disturbance	turbulance perturbed
9. post	behind/after	postpone posterity postwar	posterior postpositive
10. lūx, lūcēs (n)	light, lights	lucid lucent	translucent

Trace the Latin vocabulary words, meanings, and English derivatives below. Then add macrons!

| 1 | Word & Meaning: | vehiculum   wagon, carriage |
| | Derivatives: | vehicle, vehicular, invection |

2	Word & Meaning:	rodere, rodit, rosit
		to gnaw, (he) gnaws, (he) gnawed
	Derivatives:	erode, rodent, corrode, corrosion

| 3 | Word & Meaning: | circum   around |
| | Derivatives: | circumference, circle, circus, circumnavigate, circular |

| 4 | Word & Meaning: | certe   indeed, certainly |
| | Derivatives: | certainly, certain, uncertain, ascertain |

| 5 | Word & Meaning: | dies   day |
| | Derivatives: | diary, diurnal, journal, sundial, per diem, antemeridian, postmeridian |

6	Word & Meaning:	transire, transit, transiit
		to cross, (he) crosses, (he) crossed
	Derivatives:	transition, transit, transpose, transmit, transmission traitor, translate

| 7 | Word & Meaning: | mare   sea |
| | Derivatives: | marine, maritime, submarine, aquamarine, mare |

| 8 | Word & Meaning: | turba   crowd |
| | Derivatives: | disturb, disturbance, turbulance, perturbed |

| 9 | Word & Meaning: | post   behind/after |
| | Derivatives: | postpone, posterity, postwar, posterior, postpositive |

| 10 | Word & Meaning: | lux, luces   light, lights |
| | Derivatives: | lucid, lucent, translucent |

LESSON XI: Exercise I

Complete the sentences using English Derivatives.

FILL IN THE BLANK

CHOICES

1. He was_____he would win the race.

vehicle

2. They washed and cleaned the_____
before trying to sell it.

circumference

3. We measured the_____ of
the garden before buying plants.

erode

marine

4. The deep snow caused them to_____
their trip.

certain

5. The rain fell so hard it began to_____the
dirt.

postpone

6. Because of bad weather, we had to _____
our vacation.

transition

diary

7. We were amazed at all the_____
life in the ocean.

postpone

8. The sign said, "Do not_____."

disturb

9. He made a_____ from one job to
another.

10. She loved to write in her_____
each night before bed.

LESSON XI: Exercise II

Use a ruler. Draw a line to match the English derivative to its Latin word.

DERIVATIVE	LATIN WORD
1. diary	rōdere
2. disturb	vehiculum
3. lucid, translucent	diēs
4. rodent, erode	circum
5. marine, maritime	certē
6. vehicle	trānsīre
7. circumference, circle, circus	mare
8. transition, transit	post
9. certainly, certain	turba
10. postpone, posterity, posterior	lūx, lūcēs

LESSON XI: Exercise III

Fill in the blanks using English derivatives. Your choices are listed at the bottom of the page.

STORY

We jumped in our 1)_____ to go on our

field trip. We drove around the 2)_____ of the

fence. We were 3)_____ we could find a way in.

After all, we had been invited to attend. We 4)_____

did not want to 5)_____ our field trip.

As we rounded the last section, we saw a small gate, which opened as we came near.

We made a 6)_____ from our car to their tour

bus. We toured the facility, seeing lots of 7)_____ ,

cameras, and "Do not 8)_____ " signs.

_____

CHOICES

certainly	signs	vehicle	postpone	circumference
certain	transition	disturb		

LESSON XI: Exercise IV

What does the underlined word mean? Circle your choice.

1. We didn't want to <u>postpone</u> our trip.

    a) change   b) put off   c) plan

2. We used a string to measure the <u>circumference</u> of the candle.

    a) distance around   b) height   c) width

3. <u>Maritime</u> law tells you to be thoughtful of other sailors.

    a) marriage   b) traffic   c) sea

4. Rats and chipmunks are both in the <u>rodent</u> family.

    a) friendly   b) cute   c) small chewing

5. He was quiet so he would not <u>disturb</u> the others.

    a) bother   b) wake   c) harm

6. They made the <u>transition</u> easily from one house to the other.

    a) decision   b) a change   c) money

LESSON XI: Exercise V

Write a story using as many words from this lesson as you can. Underline the words you use.

_____

_____

_____

_____

_____

_____

_____

_____

_____

_____

_____

_____

_____

LESSON XI: Exercise VI

Circle the English derivatives in the puzzle below.

```
R Q B X T D T G T R A N S I T I O N L O
S Y G R R S N A T P D K G I M J F M M
P J M A A X U Z X M C N X F N B E C M T
M S A R N T B H B G E O X O V J O C A K
Q X S O S C M Y E N R R D J E Y B Y R F
P O C D L O A C B B T K O C C K T J I G
P X E E A T R M E H A M R B T P O Y T C
G Y R N T X I Y Q G I I C Z I O M R I O
W P T T E U N D A B N P X C O J J I M R
D V A L C P E F L K L K J G N B X N E R
S Q I V E H I C L E Y H L N S N M S J O
X F N I S D I S T U R B A N C E F R O S
P O S T E R I T Y H M N C W U P X K U I
F B C I R C U M F E R E N C E U B K R O
S E T R A N S L U C E N T C O V G C N N
O E O C I R C U M N A V I G A T E P A S
X P O S T E R I O R A X I Z D W I R L Z
D D Y O L L Q D B O N B A D V I S O R M
D V Q Q H D W W W D I A R Y I P G T P J
W D O M V I I D T U R B U L A N C E Y E
```

INVECTION	TRANSLUCENT	POSTERITY
TRANSLATE	DIARY	ADVISOR
CIRCUMFERENCE	CIRCUMNAVIGATE	SUBMARINE
DISTURBANCE	JOURNAL	RODENT
VEHICLE	MARITIME	TURBULANCE
TRANSITION	ASCERTAIN	POSTERIOR
CORROSION	CERTAINLY	

97

LESSON XII: Vocabulary

Study these Latin words, their meanings, and their English derivatives.

LATIN WORD	MEANING	DERIVATIVES	
1. perficere, perficiō, perficit, perficiēbat (v)	to complete/perform, I complete, (he) completes, (he) completed	perfect perfection	
2. mōns, montēs (n)	mountain, mountains	mount mountain mountainous surmount	tantamount dismount Montana
3. cōnsēdere, cōnsīdō, cōnsīdit, cōnsēdit (v)	to sit down, I sit down, (he) sits down, (he) sat down	president subside sedentary sediment	supersede resident session
4. discipulus, discipulī (n)	disciple, disciples	disciple discipline	
5. circumspicere, circumspiciō, circumspicit, circumspexit (v)	to look around, I look around, (he) looks around, (he) looked around	circumspect perspicacious introspection suspicion suspicious despise	suspect respect inspection aspect expect
6. emere, emit, emēbat (v)	to buy, (he) buys, (he) bought	exemption redeem	redemption
7. probāre, probō, probat, probābat (v)	to test, I test, (he) tests, (he) was testing	probable prove	approve
8. scīre, sciō, scit, scīvit (v)	to know, I know, (he) knows, (he) knew	science conscience omniscient conscientious prescient	
9. respōnsum (n)	answer	response responsible irresponsible	correspond respond
10. rēctus, rēcta, rēctum (adj) (related to regere)	correct (straight)	correct rectify	direct erect

Trace the Latin vocabulary words, meanings, and English derivatives below. Then add macrons!

1	Word & Meaning:	perficere, perficio, perficit, perficiebat
		to complete/perform, I complete, (he) completes, (he) completed
	Derivatives:	perfect, perfection
2	Word & Meaning:	mons, montes mountain, mountains
	Derivatives:	mount, mountain, mountainous, surmount,
		tantamount, dismount, Montana
3	Word & Meaning:	consedere, consido, considit, consedit
		to sit down, I sit down, (he) sits down, (he) sat down
	Derivatives:	president, subside, sedentary, sediment, supersede
		resident, session
4	Word & Meaning:	discipulus, discipuli disciple, disciples
	Derivatives:	disciple, discipline
5	Word & Meaning:	circumspicere, circumspicio, circumspicit, circumspexit
		to look around, I look around, (he) looks around,
		(he) looked around
	Derivatives:	circumspect, perspicacious, introspection, suspicion, despise
		suspicious, suspect, respect, inspection, aspect, expect
6	Word & Meaning:	emere, emit, emebat to buy, (he) buys, (he) bought
	Derivatives:	exemption, redeem, redemption
7	Word & Meaning:	probare, probo, probat, probabat
		to test, I test, (he) tests, (he) was testing
	Derivatives:	probable, approve, prove
8	Word & Meaning:	scire, scio, scit, scivit
		to know, I know, (he) knows, (he) knew
	Derivatives:	science, conscience, omniscient, conscientious, prescient
9	Word & Meaning:	responsum answer
	Derivatives:	response, responsible, irresponsible, correspond, respond
10	Word & Meaning:	rectus, recta, rectum correct (straight)
	Derivatives:	correct, rectify, direct, erect

LESSON XII: Exercise I

Complete the sentences using English Derivatives.

FILL IN THE BLANK   CHOICES

1. He wanted it to look _____ , so he   redeem
painted slowly and carefully.

                                                                    mountain
2. He gained a lot of weight because he was

_____.   perfect

3. We went to the store to_____
our coupons.   sedentary

4. He did well in the interview, so it is_____   rectify
he will get the job.

5. The_____looked beautiful with the snow   circumspectly
sparkling on it.

                                                                    conscience
6. Our_____ helps us know right from wrong.

                                                                    probable
7. When you receive an invitation, it is courteous to send a

_____.   response

8. We had to_____all our mistakes be-
fore we would be paid.   disciples

9. The_____ of Jesus followed Him
around.

10. We must walk_____if we are to
keep from falling in holes.

100

LESSON XII: Exercise II

Use a ruler. Draw a line to match the English derivative to its Latin word.

DERIVATIVE	LATIN WORD
1. sedentary	mōns
2. science, conscience	respōnsum
3. disciple, discipline	scīre
4. perfect	rēctus, -a, -um
5. mount, mountain	discipulus, discipulī
6. probable, prove, approve	circumspicere
7. correct, rectify, direct	emere
8. circumspect	cōnsīdere
9. response	probāre
10. redeem, redemption	perficere

LESSON XII: Exercise III

Fill in the blanks using English derivatives. Your choices are listed at the bottom of the page.

STORY

Tom went to the doctor because he wasn't feeling well. The doctor told him that

he needed to lose some weight. His 1)_____

lifestyle was having a big impact on his life. He needed to 2)_____

himself. His 3)_____ to the doctor was, "I will

4)_____ the situation."

Tom decided to prepare to climb the 5)_____

nearby. He wanted to 6)_____ that he could do it.

He practiced every day. He knew if he didn't live up to his word that his

7)_____ would bother him. When it came time to

climb, Tom was ready!

_____

CHOICES

conscience	rectify	sedentary	discipline	prove
mountain	response			

LESSON XII: Exercise IV

What does the underlined word mean? Circle your choice.

1. I walked <u>circumspectly</u> so I wouldn't step in front of a car.

    a) quickly   b) looking around   c) slowly

2. She led such a <u>sedentary</u> life, her mom was worried about her health.

    a) sitting still   b) exciting   c) sad

3. It is good to <u>rectify</u> any errors in the project.

    a) rearrange   b) remove   c) correct

4. He said, "I will <u>prove</u> to you I am right."

    a) convince   b) say   c) tell

5. As Christians, we believe Jesus provides <u>redemption</u> for us.

    a) forgiveness   b) gifts   c) a name

6. Since she studied hard, it is <u>probable</u> she will pass the test.

    a) unlikely   b) likely   c) definite

LESSON XII: Exercise V

Write a story using as many words from this lesson as you can. Underline the words you use.

_____

_____

_____

_____

_____

_____

_____

_____

_____

_____

_____

_____

_____

LESSON XII: Exercise VI

Choose <u>English derivatives</u> to solve the puzzle below. (Latin words are in parentheses.)

DOWN

5) a lifestyle of much sitting and little exercise (consīdere)
8) inner guide to right and wrong (scīre)
9) to put something right (rēctus, -a, -um)
10) complete, free from defects (perficere)

ACROSS

1) demonstrate the truth or existence of (probāre)
2) a large, steep hill (mōns)
3) a person thought to be guilty of a crime (circumspicere)
4) answer (respōnsum)
6) trained, controlled behavior (discipulus)
7) atone for sin (emere)

LESSON XIII: Vocabulary

Study these Latin words, their meanings, and their English derivatives.

LATIN WORD	MEANING	DERIVATIVES	
1. bonus, bona, bonum (adj), bene (adv)	good well	benefit benediction benevolence beneficial	bonafide bonus boon bountiful
2. pānis (n)	bread	pantry companion	
3. duo, duae, duo (adj)	two	duo duet	dual duel
4. vesper (n)	evening	vesper vespers (evening prayers)	
5. mille, milia (n)	one thousand, thousands	mile millennium millimeter	milliliter millipede millisecond
6. herba (n)	grass	herb herbavore	herbicide herbaceous
7. lūna (n)	moon	lunar luna loony	
8. omnēs (adj)	all	omnivorous omnipresent omnibus omnipotent omniscient	
9. contentus, contenta, contentum (adj)	satisfied (held together, happy)	content contents contain container entertain attain	retain detain entertain sustain sustenance
10. colligere (v)	to gather	collect recollect collection	

	Trace the Latin vocabulary words, meanings, and English derivatives below. Then add macrons!		
1	Word & Meaning:	bonus, bona, bonum, bene	good, well
	Derivatives:	benefit, benediction, benevolence, beneficial, bonafide, bonus boon, bountiful	
2	Word & Meaning:	panis	bread
	Derivatives:	pantry, companion	
3	Word & Meaning:	duo, duae, duo	two
	Derivatives:	duo, duet, dual, duel	
4	Word & Meaning:	vesper	evening
	Derivatives:	vesper, vespers	
5	Word & Meaning:	mille, milia	one thousand, thousands
	Derivatives:	mile, millennium, millimeter, milliliter, millipede millisecond	
6	Word & Meaning:	herba	grass
	Derivatives:	herb, herbavore, herbicide, herbaceous	
7	Word & Meaning:	luna	moon
	Derivatives:	lunar, luna, loony	
8	Word & Meaning:	omnes	all
	Derivatives:	omnivorous, omnipresent, omnibus, omnipotent, omniscient	
9	Word & Meaning:	contentus, contenta, contentum	satisfied
	Derivatives:	content, contents, contain, container, entertain, attain retain, detain, entertain, sustain, sustenance	
10	Word & Meaning:	colligere	to gather
	Derivatives:	collect, recollect, collection	

LESSON XIII: Exercise I

Complete the sentences using English Derivatives.

FILL IN THE BLANK

CHOICES

1. The third grade teacher asked Michael to

_____ the papers.

lunar

2. During church, Tom and Suzanne sang a

_____.

pantry

duet

3. The monks gathered together to say_____
before bedtime.

herbicide

4. She checked her_____ to see if she had
enough food for dinner.

collect

5. All the girls screamed when the_____
crawled out of the drain.

benediction

omniscient

6. We should be _____ with what we have.

content

7. There were so many weeds they had to use an

_____.

vespers

8. We waited late into the night to see the_____
eclipse.

millipede

9. The song "Be careful little eyes" reminds us that God is

_____.

10. At the end of the graduation, the speaker gave a

_____.

LESSON XIII: Exercise II

Use a ruler. Draw a line to match the English derivative to its Latin word.

DERIVATIVE	LATIN WORD
1. vespers	duo
2. companion, pantry	mille
3. herb, herbivore, herbicide	contentus, -a, -um
4. collect	lūna
5. omnipresent, omnipotent	pānis
6. duo, duet, dual	herba
7. loony	vesper
8. content	bonus, -a, -um
9. mile, millimeter, millipede	omnēs
10. boon	colligere

LESSON XIII: Exercise III

Fill in the blanks using English derivatives. Your choices are listed at the bottom of the page.

STORY

The zoo was having a contest to see who could 1)_____

the most insects. Contestants were paired by twos, and so were called the "Bug

2)_____." Andrew and his 3)_____

were the first to sign up. They decided to walk on a circular path around the ball field.

This proved to be 4)_____!

They were able to 5)_____several dozen

6)_____ . They were 7)_____

when the judges awarded them third place.

CHOICES

beneficial	gather	millipedes	collect	dual, duet
companion	content			

LESSON XIII: Exercise IV

What does the underlined word mean? Circle your choice.

1. They checked the <u>pantry</u> before going shopping.

      a) list   b) storeroom   c) refrigerator

2. That dinosaur was a <u>herbivore</u>.

      a) plant eater   b) meat eater   c) happy one

3. Our God is <u>omnipotent</u>.

      a) all powerful   b) all knowing   c) all present

4. He will <u>collect</u> all the fallen apples to make a pie.

      a) count   b) gather   c) share

5. The pen was 15 <u>millimeters</u> long.

      a) inches   b) a measurement smaller   c) feet
                               than an inch

6. They were <u>content</u> with the prize.

      a) disappointed   b) sad   c) satisfied

LESSON XIII: Exercise V

Write a story using as many words from this lesson as you can. Underline the words you use.

_____

_____

_____

_____

_____

_____

_____

_____

_____

_____

_____

_____

_____

_____

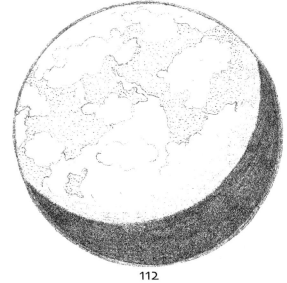

LESSON XIII: Exercise VI

Circle the English derivatives in the puzzle below.

```
N K H X B Z R Y Q U X W N L N E V B L O
I Z E N N E O A E O O K X E D X Q G O M
K R R H V W C S H L C Y P E M P X C O N
D L B E H Y L D Y V O X G N M M V L M I
C M A R D P K F Y Z M W W T I V E Z N P
L I C B I F L E H S P G I E L Q S N I O
P L E A H M I L V L A E Z R L O P K V T
Q L O V Q E G H B P N A S T E M E I O E
P I U O K L R W P L I N R A N N R H R N
A M S R D A O B G V O L A I N I S M O T
N E B E D V S U I N N O W N I S R C U A
T T H X Q J A W C O T N W U C V T S G
R E S M Q I D H B J I D Z Y M I Q T B S
Y R X J B C U Z F L R D S A I E T E H N
L Y C J G J E Z P P H I E T O N C V M C
X U E D P Y T Y A C O L L E C T I O N W
C O N T E N T E B E N E D I C T I O N F
N B T A B V E V Z E B C H Z N Z X R N O
E R K V R D U A L N W R I T X V P G L S
R W E O M N I B U S Q G G T W N B Q E K
```

LOONY
DUET
OMNIPOTENT
OMNIVOROUS
OMNISCIENT
VESPERS
OMNIBUS

HERBICIDE
DUAL
COLLECTION
HERBAVORE
LUNAR
BENEDICTION
PANTRY

CONTENT
COMPANION
MILLIMETER
MILLENNIUM
ENTERTAIN
HERBACEOUS

LESSON XIV: Vocabulary

Study these Latin words, their meanings, and their English derivatives.

Latin Word	Meaning	Derivatives	
1. remanēre, remanet, remanent (v)	to remain, stay (he) remains/stays (they) remain/stay	remain mansion permanent	remnant remainder menagerie
2. facere, facit, faciunt (v)	to do, (he) does, (they) do	fact facility sufficient	
3. plēnus, plena, plenum (adj)	full	plenty complete supply deplete	comply implement replenish
4. mīrāculum (n)	miracles	admire miracle	mirage mirror
5. caelum (n)	heavens	ceiling celestial	
6. secundus, secunda, secundum (adj)	second (in a sequence), following	second consecutive prosecute sequence	consequence suitable execute
7. sub	under	subside subtract suburb subject submarine	substandard suspend suspect sublime subjugate
8. locus (n)	place	location locate locality allow allocate	locomotive localize local dislocate
9. aridus, arida, aridum (adj)	dry	arid semiarid	
10. sēmen, sēmina (n)	seed, seeds	seminary disseminate season	seminar well-seasoned

		Trace the Latin vocabulary words, meanings, and English derivatives below. Then add macrons!
1	Word & Meaning:	remanere, remanet, remanent to remain, stay, (he) remains/stays, (they) remain/stay
	Derivatives:	remain, mansion, permanent, remnant, remainder menagerie
2	Word & Meaning:	facere, facit, faciunt to do, (he) does, (they) do
	Derivatives:	fact, facility, sufficient
3	Word & Meaning:	plenus, plena, plenum full
	Derivatives:	plenty, complete, supply, deplete, comply, implement replenish
4	Word & Meaning:	miraculum miracles
	Derivatives:	admire, miracle, mirage, mirror
5	Word & Meaning:	caelum heavens
	Derivatives:	ceiling, celestial
6	Word & Meaning:	secundus, secunda, secundum second, following
	Derivatives:	second, consecutive, prosecute, sequence, consequence, suitable, execute
7	Word & Meaning:	sub under
	Derivatives:	subside, subtract, suburb, subject, submarine, substandard suspend, suspect, sublime, subjugate
8	Word & Meaning:	locus place
	Derivatives:	location, locate, locality, allow, allocate, locomotive, localize, local, dislocate
9	Word & Meaning:	aridus, arida, aridum dry
	Derivatives:	arid, semiarid
10	Word & Meaning:	semen, semina seed, seeds
	Derivatives:	seminary, disseminate, season, seminar, well-seasoned

LESSON XIV: Exercise I

Complete the sentences using English Derivatives.

FILL IN THE BLANK

CHOICES

1. We walked through the greenhouse to_____
the flowers.

remain

facility

2. When the roof leaked, we found there was a crack in the

_____.

plenty

3. Josie was the _____child in line.

admire

4. In geography class, we tried to find the

ceiling

_____of Jerusalem.

5. We learned that the desert is very_____.

second

6. He made sure there was_____
of wood in the rack.

submarine

location

7. The man went to a_____
to study God's word.

arid

8. An officer told about his travels in a_____.

seminary

9. Will you _____, or go away?

10. The_____was closed, so we
couldn't go in.

116

LESSON XIV: Exercise II

Use a ruler. Draw a line to match the English derivative to its Latin word.

DERIVATIVE	LATIN WORD
1. plenty, complete	caelum
2. ceiling	plenus, -a, -um
3. fact, facility, sufficient	mīrāculum
4. arid	secundus, -a, -um
5. location, locate	facere
6. seminary	sub
7. admire, miracle, mirage, mirror	locus
8. second	aridus, -a, -um
9. submarine, substandard	remanēre
10. remain	sēmen

LESSON XIV: Exercise III

Fill in the blanks using English derivatives. Your choices are listed at the bottom of the page.

STORY

The students went on a field trip to the desert. They made sure to have

1)_____water. There was 2)_____

of sand all around. The air was very 3)_____. A goal of the

field trip was to 4)_____ as many different species of plants

as they could. The students had heard about seeing things not really there, but were

surprised to actually see a 5)_____. They had such a

good time, they wanted to 6)_____ , but at four

o'clock it was time to go.

CHOICES

arid	mirage	sufficient	remain	locate
plenty				

LESSON XIV: Exercise IV

What does the underlined word mean? Circle your choice.

1. Because <u>substandard</u> material was used, the bridge collapsed.

    a) solid   b) below normal   c) superior

2. The <u>facility</u> was closed for repairs.

    a) refrigerator   b) flour   c) building

3. We will try to <u>locate</u> the best place for our vacation.

    a) land   b) find   c) purchase

4. She will <u>remain</u> in the hospital for a few days.

    a) visit   b) go   c) stay

5. We <u>admired</u> the paintings.

    a) looked at with pleasure   b) bought   c) sold

6. The weather in Arizona is very <u>arid</u>.

    a) dry   b) wet   c) humid

LESSON XIV: Exercise V

Write a story using as many words from this lesson as you can. Underline the words you use.

_____

_____

_____

_____

_____

_____

_____

_____

_____

_____

_____

_____

_____

_____

_____

LESSON XIV: Exercise VI

Choose <u>English derivatives</u> to solve the puzzle below. (Latin words are in parentheses.)

DOWN

3) a ministry college (sēmen)
4) a train engine (locus)
5) after the first (secundus, -a, -um)
8) an act of God (mīrāculum)
10) enough (facere)

ACROSS

1) continue to exist (remanēre)
2) an underwater vessel (sub)
6) the upper surface of a room (caelum)
7) more than enough (plenus, -a, -um)
9) dry (aridus, -a, -um)

LESSON XV: Vocabulary

Study these Latin words, their meanings, and their English derivatives.

Latin Word	Meaning	Derivatives		
1. frūgēs (n)	fruits, crops	frugal fruitful unfruitful	grapefruit fruit	fructose fruition
2. signum (n)	sign	sign signify signal significant	signature resigned design unsigned	reassign assign consign
3. tempus, tempora (n)	season, seasons	temporary temporal contemporary extemporaneous	distemper tempest temperature	tense temperance tempura
4. annus (n)	year	annual annals Anno Domini anniversary	biannual biennial per annum	
5. maīor	greater	mayor majority	major majestic	
6. minōr	lesser, smaller	minor minority	miniscule	
7. stella (n)	star	constellation stellar	interstellar	
8. quartus, quarta, quartum (adj)	fourth	quart quarter quarry quarterback	quadruple quadruped quarantine quartet	
9. dīvidere (v)	to divide	divide dividend subdivide divisible	device devise individual	
10. terra	earth	territory terrain terra firma terrapin	terrestrial inter interment	

Trace the Latin vocabulary words, meanings, and English derivatives below. Then add macrons!			

1	Word & Meaning:	fruges	fruits, crops
	Derivatives:	frugal, fruitful, unfruitful, grapefruit, fruit, fructose fruition	

2	Word & Meaning:	signum	sign
	Derivatives:	sign, signify, signal, significant, signature, resigned design, unsigned, reassign, assign, consign	

3	Word & Meaning:	tempus, tempora	season, seasons
	Derivatives:	temporary, temporal, contemporary, extemporaneous distemper, tempest, temperature, tense, temperance, tempura	

4	Word & Meaning:	annus	year
	Derivatives:	annual, annals, Anno Domini, anniversary, biannual biennial, per annum	

5	Word & Meaning:	maior	greater
	Derivatives:	mayor, majority, major, majestic	

6	Word & Meaning:	minor	lesser, smaller
	Derivatives:	minor, minority, miniscule	

7	Word & Meaning:	stella	star
	Derivatives:	constellation, stellar, interstellar	

8	Word & Meaning:	quartus, quarta, quartum	fourth
	Derivatives:	quart, quarter, quarry, quarterback, quadruple, quadruped, quarantine, quartet	

9	Word & Meaning:	dividere	to divide
	Derivatives:	divide, dividend, subdivide, divisible, device, devise individual	

10	Word & Meaning:	terra	earth
	Derivatives:	territory, terrain, terra firma, terrapin, terrestrial inter, interment	

LESSON XV: Exercise I

Complete the sentences using English Derivatives.

FILL IN THE BLANK   CHOICES

1. Living in the small house was only_____.   major

2. The number twenty is _____   sign
by ten, five, two, and one.

3. The carpenter said there would need only   terrain

_____ repairs.

temporary
4. The earthquake caused_____
damage to the bridge.

divisible

5. Orion is the name of a _____.

annual

6. There are four_____
in a gallon.   minor

7. Because she is so_____, she is   quart
able to save money every month.

frugal
8. We planted both_____ and
perennial flowers.

constellation

9. We looked for some_____ in the grass
that the deer had been here.

10. The_____was dry and dusty
because no rain had come.

LESSON XV: Exercise II

Use a ruler. Draw a line to match the English derivative to its Latin word.

DERIVATIVE	LATIN WORD
1. constellation, stellar	signum
2. frugal	annus
3. quart, quarter	tempus
4. sign, signify, signal, significant	frūgēs
5. devise	maīor
6. annual, annals	minōr
7. territory, terrain, terrestrial	stella
8. mayor, majority	quartus, -a, -um
9. temporary, temporal, contemporary	dīvidere
10. minor, minority	terra

LESSON XV: Exercise III

Fill in the blanks using English derivatives. Your choices are listed at the bottom of the page.

STORY

Tom and Mary decided to plant a garden. They didn't have much money, so they

had to be 1)_____ with their money.

They drove 2) _____ to different nurseries. They were

careful to check all the 3)_____ for sales. Hoping to stay in

their budget, they bought some perennials and some 4)_____.

They realized that the annuals were beautiful but 5)_____,

since they only lasted one season. At the end of their shopping, they were delighted

that they had only spent a 6)_____of their

budget! That left them with the 7)_____ of their money

to spend another day!

CHOICES

annuals	individually	frugal	temporary	majority
signs	quarter			

LESSON XV: Exercise IV

What does the underlined word mean? Circle your choice.

1. The candy was <u>divided</u> into three parts.

   a) multiplies   b) separated   c) melted

2. A <u>quarter</u> of the snow had been removed.

   a) one fourth   b) one third   c) one half

3. As we looked at the desert, we could see the <u>terrain</u> was dry and dusty.

   a) land   b) air   c) water

4. The seed company produced an <u>annual</u> catalog.

   a) free   b) monthly   c) yearly

5. Susan was a <u>frugal</u> person.

   a) faithful   b) careful (of money)   c) foolish

6. A green light usually <u>signifies</u> "to go."

   a) means, shows   b) warm   c) helps

LESSON XV: Exercise V

Write a story using as many words from this lesson as you can. Underline the words you use.

_____

_____

_____

_____

_____

_____

_____

_____

_____

_____

_____

_____

_____

_____

_____

LESSON XV: Exercise VI

Circle the English derivatives in the puzzle below.

```
T  Z  V  E  Z  P  Q  T  R  M  M  I  N  I  S  C  U  L  E  V
F  R  U  C  T  O  S  E  E  G  V  C  E  Q  T  E  G  G  X  O
C  T  J  I  Z  I  V  W  J  P  L  S  D  O  X  U  B  A  T  D
T  E  P  S  I  G  N  I  F  Y  X  M  R  V  M  Y  D  N  E  F
Q  R  U  G  V  T  M  T  O  T  W  K  S  D  I  M  Q  N  M  O
U  R  T  L  R  T  E  W  E  P  P  V  H  Q  N  N  E  U  P  U
A  E  U  I  P  A  O  M  L  R  D  L  G  Z  O  O  X  A  O  S
R  S  X  M  D  U  P  P  P  D  S  P  T  R  R  G  V  L  R  I
A  T  Q  U  A  R  T  E  R  O  H  T  P  Y  I  E  M  S  A  G
N  R  W  W  B  Q  A  G  F  M  R  H  E  U  T  G  K  T  N  N
T  I  S  V  L  X  B  Q  Z  R  A  A  Y  L  Y  J  C  M  E  I
I  A  P  N  F  L  H  V  Z  N  U  J  R  I  L  L  N  Y  O  F
N  L  T  E  R  R  I  T  O  R  Y  I  E  Y  T  A  E  Z  U  I
E  V  V  W  M  R  I  X  O  L  I  B  T  S  S  E  R  L  S  C
Q  X  N  V  O  P  L  J  U  W  V  J  J  I  T  N  G  A  X  A
O  W  A  N  N  I  V  E  R  S  A  R  Y  E  N  I  M  M  V  N
W  K  E  R  X  U  Z  R  V  H  J  R  U  I  U  M  C  A  F  T
H  S  I  G  N  A  T  U  R  E  Q  F  R  U  G  A  L  B  M  W
R  E  C  O  N  S  T  E  L  L  A  T  I  O  N  U  K  L  K  S
J  A  D  E  R  C  Q  K  I  M  A  J  O  R  I  T  Y  M  B  S
```

FRUGAL	SIGNIFY	ANNUAL
TERRITORY	MINORITY	TERRESTRIAL
TEMPORARY	FRUCTOSE	MAJESTIC
QUARANTINE	CONSTELLATION	QUARTER
GRAPEFRUIT	ANNIVERSARY	INTERSTELLAR
SIGNATURE	EXTEMPORANEOUS	MINISCULE
MAJORITY	SIGNIFICANT	

REVIEW: Part I

Write one English derivative for each Latin word from Lessons XI-XV. (Multiple possible answers!)

LATIN WORD	DERIVATIVE	LATIN WORD	DERIVATIVE
1. quartus, -a, -um	_____	11. plēnus, -a, -um	_____
2. cōnsīdere	_____	12, rodere	_____
3. facere	_____	13. locus	_____
4. mare	_____	14. probāre	_____
5. secundus, -a, -um	_____	15. mille	_____
6. circumspicere	_____	16. frūges	_____
7. tempus	_____	17. turba	_____
8. respōnsum	_____	18. terra	_____
9. sēmen	_____	19. annus	_____
10. duō	_____	20. herba	_____

REVIEW: Part II

Write ten sentences using the derivatives you listed on Page 130.

1. _____

_____

2. _____

_____

3. _____

_____

4. _____

_____

5. _____

_____

6. _____

_____

7. _____

_____

8. _____

_____

9. _____

_____

10. _____

_____

LATIN PREFIXES

LATIN PREFIX	MEANING
1. ā, ab	away from
2. ad	toward
3. com, con, cor	together
4. di, dis	apart
5. dē	down from
6. ex	out of
7. in	in, not
8. inter	between, among
9. intrā	inside, within
10. oc, op, ob	up against
11. omni	all
12. pen	almost
13. per	through
14. post	after
15. pre	before
16. pro	forward
17. re, retro	backwards
18. sub	under
19. super	above, over
20. trans	across
21. uni	one
22. via	by way of

PREFIX WORKSHEET

Identify the English Derivative we get by combining the following Latin prefixes and root word.

<u>LATIN PREFIXES</u>   DERIVATIVE

1. com (together) + ponit (he places)   _____

2 de (down from) + mōtum (motion)   _____

3. in (not) + finite   _____

4. in (not) + frangible (breakable)   _____

5. in (not) + vulnera (wounded) + able (able to be) _____

6. inter (between) + venit (he comes)   _____

7. inter (between) + lūdit (he plays)   _____

8. inter (between) + captivus (capture)   _____

9. omni (all) + potent (powerful)   _____

10. post (after) + ponit (he places)   _____

11. pro (forward) + mōtum (motion)   _____

12. re (backwards) + linquit (leave)   _____

13. re (backwards) + vivit (alive)   _____

14. uni (one) + cycle   _____

15. via (by way of) + duct   _____

VOCABULARY

Below find each of the Latin words in Derivatives I listed alphabetically with its definition and the Lesson in which it appears.

afflictus, a, um: discouraged (Lesson V)
alter: another (Lesson III)
altus, a, um: high (Lesson VI)
ambulare: to walk (Lesson VIII)
animal: animal (Lesson III)
annus: year (Lesson VI)
aperire: to open (Lesson X)
apparere: to appear (Lesson VII)
aqua: water (Lesson IV)
aridus, a, um: dry (Lesson XIV)
audire: to hear (Lesson II)
auxilium: help (noun) (Lesson VIII)
benedicere: to bless (Lesson XIII)
beneficium: a favor, good deed (Lesson X)
bonus: good (Lesson XIII)
capere: to catch (Lesson X)
captivus: captive (Lesson VI)
caelum: heavens (Lesson XIV)
carcer: prison (Lesson VII)
caudam: tail (Lesson VII)
centum: one hundred (Lesson V)
cetera: all the others (Lesson III)
certe: indeed (Lesson XI)
circum: around (Lesson XI)
circiter: approximately (Lesson XIII)
circumspicere: to look around (Lesson XII)
clamare: to shout (Lesson VII)
colligere: to gather (Lesson XIII)
consistere: to stop (Lesson VIII)
considere: to sit down (Lesson XII)
contentus: satisfied (Lesson XIII)
curare: to take care of (Lesson IX)
currere: to run (Lesson II)
cursus: a race (Lesson III)
dare: to give (Lesson VIII)
descendere: to come down (Lesson VII)
desertum: desert (noun) (Lesson V)
dicere: to say (Lesson I)
dies: day (Lesson XI)
discipulus: disciple (Lesson XII)
dīvidere: to divide (Lesson XV)
domus: home (Lesson VI)
dormire: to sleep (Lesson IV)
duo, duae, duo: two (Lesson XIII)

ducere: to lead (Lesson IX)
edere: to eat (Lesson X)
ego: I (Lesson VI)
emere: to buy (Lesson XII)
evertere: to turn upside down (Lesson V)
excitare: to excite (Lesson III)
exire: to go out (Lesson I)
facere: to make/do (Lesson XIV)
finis: end (Lesson IV)
firmus, a, um: strong (Lesson V)
formica: ant (Lesson VI)
frangere: to break into pieces (Lesson V)
fruges: fruits, crops (Lesson XV)
gradus: step (Lesson IV)
gravis, gravis, grave: heavy (Lesson V)
herba: grass (Lesson XIII)
homo: man (Lesson VII)
imponere: to place on (Lesson VI)
infudere: to pour over (Lesson IX)
initium: beginning (Lesson III)
intrare: to enter (Lesson II)
invenire: to find (Lesson IV)
leo: lion (Lesson X)
liber, a, um: free (Lesson X)
ligare: to tie (Lesson X)
locus: place (Lesson XIV)
ludere: to play (Lesson VI)
lustrāre: to shine light on (Lesson X)
lūx, lumen: light (Lesson XI)
magnus, a, um: large (Lesson I)
maior: greater (Lesson XV)
malus, a, um: bad (Lesson I)
mare: sea (Lesson XI)
mater: mother (Lesson I)
maxime: very much (Lesson IV)
mille: thousand (Lesson XIII)
minime: no way (Lesson V)
minor: lesser (Lesson XV)
miraculum: miracle (Lesson XIV)
mons: mountain (Lesson XII)
motus: motion (Lesson VI)
necesse: necessary (Lesson II
noctem: night (Lesson IX)
nomināre: to name (Lesson VIII)

VOCABULARY

obscura: dark, hidden (Lesson VIII)
oculi: eyes (Lesson IV)
oleum: oil (Lesson IX)
omnes: all (Lesson XIII)
panis: bread (Lesson XIII)
perficere: to complete (Lesson XII)
pes: foot, paw (Lesson X)
plenus: full (Lesson XIV)
porcus: pig (Lesson II)
portare: to carry (Lesson I)
posse: is able (Lesson V)
post: behind, after (Lesson XI)
primus, a , um: first (Lesson I)
probare: to test (Lesson XII)
prope: near (Lesson IX)
proximus, a, u: next (Lesson IX)
provocare: to challenge (Lesson III)
prudens: wise (Lesson II)
quaerere: to look for (Lesson VI)
quartus: fourth (Lesson XV)
rapidissimus, a, um: very fast (Lesson II)
rectus: correct (Lesson XII)
relinquere: to leave behind (Lesson V)
remanere: to remain (Lesson XIV)
respondere: to respond (Lesson II)
responsum: answer (noun) (Lesson XII)
rex, regere: king/to rule (Lesson X)
rodere: to gnaw (Lesson XI)
sacerdos: priest (Lesson VIII)
satis: enough (Lesson IV)
scire: to know (Lesson XII)
secundus: second (Lesson XIV)
semen: plants (Lesson XIV)
silva: forest (Lesson III)
signum: sign (Lesson XV)
sol: sunshine (Lesson VI)
solus, sola, solum: only (Lesson VII)
stella: star (Lesson XV)
sub: under (Lesson XIV)
stabulum: stable (Lesson IX)
superare: to overcome (Lesson (III)
suspicere: to look up (Lesson VII)
tardus, a, um: slow (Lesson IV)
tempus: season (Lesson XV)

terra: earth (Lesson XV)
transire: to cross (Lesson XI)
tres, tres, tria: three (Lesson I)
turba: crowd (Lesson XI)
umbra: shadow (Lesson VII)
unus, una, unum: one (Lesson III)
vacuus, a, um: empty (Lesson VII)
vehiculum: wagon (Lesson XI)
velle: to want (Lesson I)
verberare: to beat (Lesson VIII)
venire: to respond (Lesson II)
vesper: evening (Lesson XIII)
via: road (Lesson VIII)
videre: to see (Lesson I)
vinum: wine (Lesson IX)
vivus, a, um: alive (Lesson VI)
villa: house (Lesson II)
volare: to fly (Lesson VII)
vulnus: wound (Lesson X)

135

ANSWER KEY: LESSON I

LESSON II

FILL IN THE BLANK, p.8

1. dictionary
2. porter
3. magnify
4. diction
5. malicious
6. exit
7. primary
8. volunteer
9. video
10. triangle

STORY, p. 10

1. porter
2. diction
3. large
4. malice
5. vounteer

FILL IN THE BLANK, p. 16

1. introduce
2. necessary
3. pork
4. respond
5. auditorium
6. prudent
7. current
8. village
9. Advent

STORY, p. 18

1. response
2. villa
3. introduce
4. necessary
5. pork
6. prudent
7. current

MATCHING, p. 9

1. dictionary--dicere
2. three--trēs, trēs, tria
3. portable--portāre
4. volunteer--velle
5. magnify--magnus, magna, magnum
6. exit--exīre
7. malice--malus, mala, malum
8. first--primus, prima, primum
9. video--videre
10. maternity--māter

MULTIPLE CHOICE, p. 11

1. c
2. c
3. b
4. b
5. c
6. a
7. b

MATCHING, p. 17

1. necessary--necesse
2. pork, porcupine--porcus, porcī
3. respond--respondere
4. advent--venīre
5. house--vīlla
6. current--currere
7. rapid--rapidissimus, -a, -um
8. introduce--intrāre
9. prudent--prūdēns
10. auditorium--audīre

MULTIPLE CHOICE, p. 19

1. b
2. c
3. c
4. a
5. b
6. b

PUZZLE, P. 13

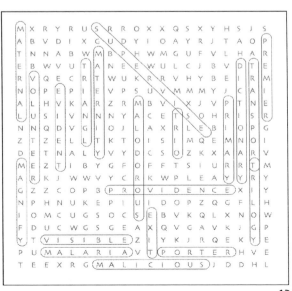

PUZZLE, P. 21

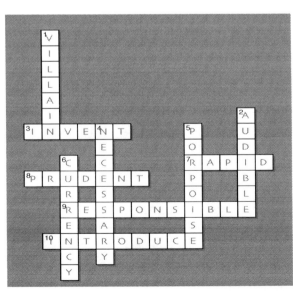

ANSWER KEY: LESSON III

LESSON IV

Lesson III

<u>FILL IN THE BLANK, P. 24</u>

1. initials
2. a course
3. alternate, alternative
4. provoke
5. animals
6. Pennsylvania
7. Superman
8. United
9. excited
10. et cetera

<u>STORY, P. 26</u>

1. course
2. Initially
3. excited
4. united
5. alternate
6. animals
7. forest

<u>MATCHING, P. 25</u>

1. animal--animāl
2. a course--cursus
3. initials, initial--initiūm
4. one--ūnus, ūna, ūnum
5. superman--superāre
6. excite--excitāre, excitābat
7. et cetera--cētera
8. he provokes, provoked, prōvocāre, provocāvit
9. alternative, alternate--altera
10. Pennsylvania--silva

<u>MULTIPLE CHOICE, P. 27</u>

1. a
2. b
3. c
4. b
5. a

Lesson IV

<u>FILL IN THE BLANK, P. 32</u>

1. invent
2. satisfied
3. tardy
4. gradually
5. aquarium
6. maximum
7. binoculars
8. altitude
9. finish
10. dormitory

<u>STORY, P. 34</u>

1. tardy
2. aquarium
3. binoculars
4. altitude
5. satisfied
6. maximum

<u>MATCHING, P. 33</u>

1. grade, gradual--gradus,
2. tardy--tardus, tarda, tardum
3. satisfy, satisfaction--satis
4. altitude--altus, alta, altum
5. binoculars--oculī
6. maximum--maximē
7. dormitory--dormīre
8. finish--finis
9. invent--invenīre
10. aquarium--aqua

<u>MULTIPLE CHOICE, P. 35</u>

1. b
2. b
3. c
4. c
5. b
6. a

<u>PUZZLE, P. 29</u>

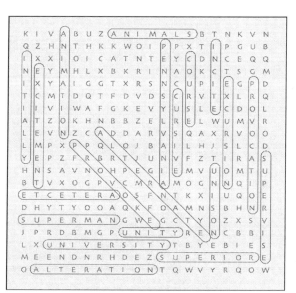

<u>PUZZLE, P. 37</u>

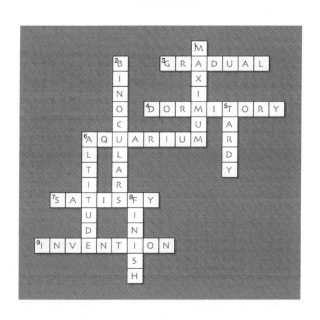

ANSWER KEY: LESSON V

FILL IN THE BLANK, P.40

1. invert
2. potential
3. desert
4. gravity
5. minimum
6. firm
7. cents
8. fraction
9. relinquish

STORY, P. 42

1. century
2. gravity
3. fraction
4. advertisement
5. minimum
6. firm
7. relinquish
8. century

MATCHING, P. 41

1. to afflict--afflictus, -a, -um
2. firm--firmus, -a, -um
3. potential--posse
4. gravity--gravis, gravis, grave
5. fraction, fracture--frangere
6. relic, relinquish--relinquere
7. century, percent, cent--centum
8. minimum--minimē
9. advertise, invert, divert, revert--ēvertere
10. desert--desertum

MULTIPLE CHOICE, P. 43

1. b
2. a
3. c
4. c
5. a

PUZZLE, P. 45

REVIEW PAGE, P. 46

(Multiple answers possible from Lessons I-V)

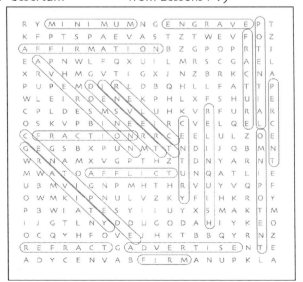

LESSON VI

FILL IN THE BLANK, P. 50

1. formica
2. motion
3. inquire
4. egotist
5. capture
6. vivacious
7. impose
8. ludicrous
9. solar
10. dome

STORY, P. 52

1. solar
2. postpone
3. inquire
4. egotist
5. capture
6. domesticated

MATCHING, P. 51

1. acquire, inquire--quaerere
2. motion--mōtus
3. impose--impōnere
4. domesticated, dome, dominate--domus
5. solar--sōl
6. capture--captīvus
7. formica--formīca
8. vivacious--vīvus, -a, -um
9. egotist--ego
10. elude, ludicrous--lūdere

MULTIPLE CHOICE, P. 53

1. b
2. a
3. c
4. b
5. b
6. c

PUZZLE, P. 55

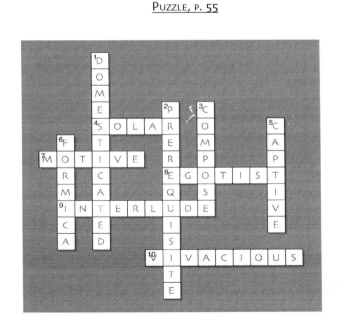

138

ANSWER KEY: LESSON VII

FILL IN THE BLANK, P. 58

1. vacation
2. umbrella
3. appear
4. solitary
5. vacant
6. homicides
7. suspect
8. incarcerated
9. volatile
10. clamor

STORY, P. 60

1. homicide
2. suspicion
3. vacant
4. exclaimed
5. appeared
6. incarcerated
7. solitary

MATCHING, P. 59

1. incarcerate--carcer
2. clamor--clāmāre
3. sole, solitary, solitaire, desolation--sōlus, -a, -um
4. apparition, appear--appārēre
5. homicide--homō
6. coda--cauda
7. umbrella--umbra
8. vacant, vacation--vacuus, -a, -um
9. suspicion--suspicere
10. volatile--volāre

MULTIPLE CHOICE, P. 61

1. a
2. c
3. b
4. b
5. b

PUZZLE, P. 63

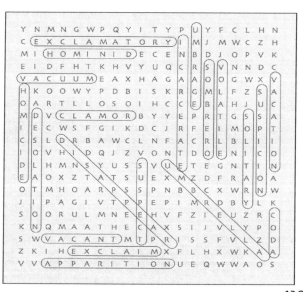

LESSON VIII

FILL IN THE BLANK, P. 66

1. descended
2. nominated
3. sacrifice
4. reverberated
5. via
6. consistently
7. ambulance
8. auxiliary
9. obscured
10. dedicated

STORY, P. 68

1. ascend
2. deviate
3. consistent
4. obscure
5. descend
6. reverberate

MATCHING, P. 67

1. sacred, sacrifice--sacerdōs
2. via, deviate--via
3. dark, hidden--obscura
4. descend--dēscendere
5. dedicate--dare, dat, dedit
6. amble, ambulance--ambulāre, ambulābat
7. nominate--nomināre
8. consistent--constitere, constitit
9. auxiliary--auxilium
10. reverberate--verberare, verberāvērunt

MULTIPLE CHOICE, P. 69

1. c
2. a
3. b
4. a
5. a
6. c

PUZZLE, P. 71

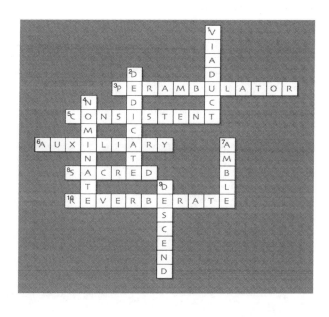

139

ANSWER KEY: LESSON IX

FILL IN THE BLANK, P. 74

1. oil
2. produce
3. approached
4. approximately
5. vine
6. wine
7. stable
8. curator
9. vulnerable
10. nocturnal

STORY, P. 76

1. approximately
2. approached
3. stable
4. vulnerable
5. conductor
6. oil

MATCHING, P. 75

1. infuse, infusion--īnfūdere
2. wine, vine--vīnum
3. conductor, reduce, induce, produce--dūcere, dūcit, dūxit
4. approach--prope
5. vulnerable, invulnerable--vulnus
6. approximate--proximus, -a, -um
7. oil--oleum
8. nocturnal--noctem
9. stable--stabulum
10. curator--cūrāre

MULTIPLE CHOICE, P. 77

1. c
2. a
3. a
4. b
5. a
6. b

PUZZLE, P. 79

LESSON X

FILL IN THE BLANK, P. 82

1. benefactor
2. lion
3. pedestrian
4. April
5. Leo
6. edible
7. reigned
8. liberty
9. captive
10. ligament

STORY, P. 84

1. April
2. captured
3. liberated
4. benefactor
5. edible
6. illustrated
7. royalty

MATCHING, P. 83

1. illustrate--lustrāre
2. edible--edere
3. benefactor--beneficium
4. Leo--leō
5. pedal, pedestrian, pedestal--pēs
6. ligament--ligāre
7. regal, reign--rēx, regere
8. April--aperīre, aperit, aperuit
9. liberty, liberate, liberal--līber, -a, -um
10. capture, accept, captive--capere

MULTIPLE CHOICE, P. 85

1. c
2. a
3. a
4. b
5. a
6. b

PUZZLE, P. 87

REVIEW PAGE, P. 88

(Multiple answers possible from Lessons VI-X)

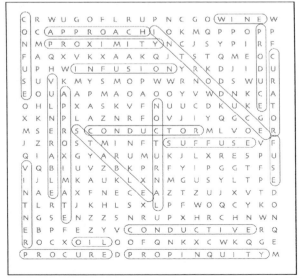

ANSWER KEY: LESSON XI

LESSON XII

FILL IN THE BLANK, P. 92

1. certain
2. vehicle
3. circumference
4. postpone
5. erode
6. postpone
7. marine
8. disturb
9. transition
10. diary

STORY, P. 94

1. vehicle
2. circumference
3. certain
4. certainly
5. postpone
6. transition
7. signs
8. disturb

FILL IN THE BLANK, P. 100

1. perfect
2. sedentary
3. redeem
4. probable
5. mountain
6. conscience
7. response
8. rectify
9. disciples
10. circumspectly

STORY, P. 102

1. sedentary
2. discipline
3. response
4. rectify
5. mountain
6. prove
7. conscience

MATCHING, P. 93

1. diary--diēs
2. disturb--turba
3. lucid, translucent--lūx, lūces
4. rodent, erode--rōdere
5. marine, maritime--mare
6. vehicle--vehiculum
7. circumference, circle, cir-cus--circum
8. transition, transit--trānsīre
9. certainly, certain--certē
10. postpone, posterity, posterior--post

MULTIPLE CHOICE, P. 95

1. b
2. a
3. c
4. c
5. a
6. b

MATCHING, P. 101

1. sedentary--cōnsīdere
2. science, conscience-scīre
3. disciple, discipline--discipulus, discipulī
4. perfect--perficit, perficēre
5. mount, mountain--mōns
6. probable, prove, approve--probāre
7. correct, rectify, direct--rēctus, -a, -um
8. circumspect--circumspicere
9. response--respōnsum
10. redeem, redemption--emere

MULTIPLE CHOICE, P. 103

1. b
2. a
3. c
4. a
5. a
6. b

PUZZLE, P. 97

PUZZLE, P. 105

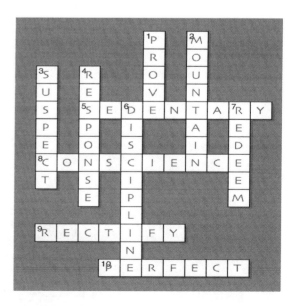

ANSWER KEY: LESSON XIII

FILL IN THE BLANK, P. 108

1. collect
2. duet
3. vespers
4. pantry
5. millipede
6. content
7. herbicide
8. lunar
9. omniscient
10. benediction

STORY, P. 110

1. collect/gather
2. Duet
3. companion
4. beneficial
5. collect/gather
6. millipedes
7. content

MATCHING, P. 109

1. vespers--vesper
2. companion, pantry--pānis
3. herb, herbivore, herbicide--herba
4. collect--colligere
5. omnipresent, omnipresent--omnēs
6. duo, duet, dual--duo
7. loony--lūna
8. content--contentus, -a, -um
9. mile, millimeter, millipede--mille
10. boon--bonus, -a, -um

MULTIPLE CHOICE, P. 111

1. b
2. a
3. a
4. b
5. b
6. c

PUZZLE, P. 113

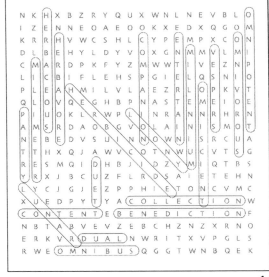

LESSON XIV

FILL IN THE BLANK, P. 116

1. admire
2. ceiling
3. second
4. location
5. arid
6. plenty
7. seminary
8. submarine
9. remain
10. facility

STORY, P. 118

1. sufficient
2. plenty
3. arid
4. locate
5. mirage
6. remain

MATCHING, P. 117

1. plenty, complete--plēnus, -a, -um
2. ceiling--caelum
3. fact, facility, sufficient--facere
4. arid--aridus, -a, -um
5. location, locate--locus
6. seminary--sēmina
7. admire, miracle, mirage, mirror--mīrāculum
8. second--secundus, -a, -um
9. submarine, substandard--sub
10. remain--remanēre

MULTIPLE CHOICE, P. 119

1. b
2. c
3. b
4. c
5. a
6. a

PUZZLE, P. 121

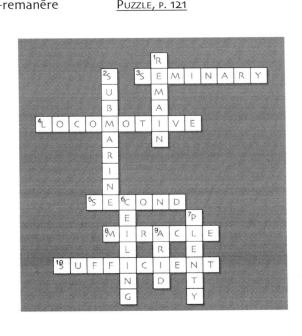

ANSWER KEY: LESSON XV

PREFIX WORKSHEET

1. temporary
2. divisible
3. minor
4. major
5. constellation
6. quarts
7. frugal
8. annual
9. sign
10. terrain

STORY, P. 126

1. frugal
2. individually
3. signs
4. annuals
5. temporary
6. quarter
7. majority

PAGE 133

1. compose
2. demote
3. infinite
4. infrangible
5. invulnerable
6. intervene
7. interlude
8. intercept
9. omnipotent
10. postpone
11. promote
12. relinquish
13. revive
14. unicycle
15. viaduct

MATCHING, P. 125

1. constellation, stellar--stella
2. frugal--frūgēs
3. quart, quarter--quartus, -a, -um
4. sign, signify, signal, significant--signum
5. devise--dīvidere
6. annual, annals--annus
7. territory, terrain, terrestrial--terra
8. mayor, majority--maīor
9. temporary, temporal, contemporary--tempus
10. minor, minority--minōr

MULTIPLE CHOICE, P. 127

1. b
2. a
3. a
4. c
5. b
6. a

PUZZLE, P. 129

REVIEW PAGE, P. 130

(Multiple answers possible from Lessons XI-XV)

143

Items available from Laurelwood Books:

Ōlim, Once Upon a Time, in Latin Series:
Book I (reader and workbook): The Three Little Pigs, The Tortoise and the Hare,
The Crow and the Pitcher
Book II (reader and workbook): The Ant and the Chrysalis, The Lost Sheep,
The Good Samaritan
Book III (reader and workbook) - The Feeding of the 5,000,The Lion and the Mouse
Book IV (reader and workbook) - Creation
Book V (reader and workbook) - Daniel, Part I; We Know a Tree by its Fruit
Book VI (reader and workbook) - The Prodigal Son
book VII (reader and workbook) - David and Goliath
Book VIII (reader and workbook) - Daniel, Part II
Book IX (reader and workbook) - Daniel, Part III, The Miser
Book X (reader and workbook) - The Wise Man and Foolish Man, The Ten Maidens

Ōlim Derivatives I
Ōlim Derivatives II (Coming Soon)

Scripture Scribes Series
Primary (Coming Soon)
Intermediate: *One Another*
Upper School (Coming Soon)

Patriotic Penmanship Series for Grades K-12
Also Available: Jump Rope Review Book, Transition to Cursive Book,
Dinosaur Review Book

State The Facts: A Guide to Studying Your State Whether you are studying the state you
live in or any other state, this book offers your student the opportunity to research and
learn state history, geography, weather, and more!

Study Guides:
Based on Rosemary Sutcliff's historical fiction
The Eagle of the Ninth • The Silver Branch Outcast • The Lantern Bearers
Warrior Scarlet • Sword Song • The Shining Company

Based on Emma Leslie's historical fiction:
Out of the Mouth of the Lion
Glaucia the Greek Slave

Laurelwood Books offers both new and used curricula to families wishing
to help their children learn and achieve success in school or at home.

To order: www.laurelwoodbooks.com
laurelwoodbooks@earthlink.net

Made in the USA
San Bernardino, CA
09 April 2016